Wells Brothers
The Young Cattle Kings

by

Andy Adams

Wells Brothers
The Young Cattle King
by Andy Adams

Copyright © 2023

All Rights reserved.

No part of this publication may be reproduced, stored in a retrieval system, or transmitted in any form or by any means, electronic, mechanical, photocopying or Otherwise, without the written permission of the publisher.
The author/editor asserts the moral right to be identified as the author/editor of this work.

ISBN: 978-93-58595-44-4

Published by
DOUBLE 9 BOOKS
2/13-B, Ansari Road
Daryaganj, New Delhi – 110002
info@double9books.com
www.double9books.com
Tel. 011-40042856

This book is under public domain

ABOUT THE AUTHOR

Andy Adams was an American author of western literature who lived from May 3, 1859, to September 26, 1935. The son of Andrew Adams, who was of Irish origin, and Elizabeth Elliott, who was of Scottish descent, Andy Adams was born in Thorncreek Township, Whitley County, Indiana. He assisted with the cattle and horses on the family farm when he was a little boy. He moved to Texas in the early 1880s and lived there for ten years, spending a lot of that time moving cattle over the western routes. He attempted to become a merchant in 1890, but the endeavor was unsuccessful. He next tried his hand at gold mining in Colorado and Nevada. He relocated to Colorado Springs in 1894, where he remained until his death. His most popular work, The Log of a Cowboy, was published in 1903, when he was 43 years old and he starting to write. A Texas Matchmaker (1904), The Outlet (1905), Cattle Brands (1906), Reed Anthony, Cowman: An Autobiography (1907), Wells Brothers (1911), and The Ranch on the Beaver are some of his other books (1927).

CONTENTS

CHAPTER I.
WAIFS OF THE PLAIN 7

CHAPTER II.
THE HOSPITAL ON THE BEAVER 14

CHAPTER III.
THE BOTTOM RUNG 23

CHAPTER IV.
THE BROTHERS CLAIM A RANGE 31

CHAPTER V.
A FALL OF CRUMBS 39

CHAPTER VI.
SUNSHINE AND SHADOW 46

CHAPTER VII.
ALL IN THE DAY'S WORK 54

CHAPTER VIII.
THE LINES OF INTRENCHMENT 61

CHAPTER IX.
A WINTRY CRUCIBLE 69

CHAPTER X.
GOOD FIGHTING 77

CHAPTER XI.
HOLDING THE FORT 85

CHAPTER XII.
    A WINTER DRIFT 93

CHAPTER XIII.
    A WELCOME GUEST 102

CHAPTER XIV.
    AN ILL WIND 108

CHAPTER XV.
    WATER! WATER! 115

CHAPTER XVI.
    A PROTECTED CREDIT 123

CHAPTER XVII.
    "THE WAGON" 131

CHAPTER XVIII.
    AN OPEN WINTER 137

CHAPTER XIX.
    AN INDIAN SCARE 145

CHAPTER XX.
    HARVEST ON THE RANGE 151

CHAPTER XXI.
    LIVING IN THE SADDLE 160

CHAPTER XXII.
    INDEPENDENCE 168

CHAPTER I.
WAIFS OF THE PLAIN

The first herd of trail cattle to leave Dodge City, Kansas, for the Northwest, during the summer of 1885, was owned by the veteran drover, Don Lovell. Accidents will happen, and when about midway between the former point and Ogalalla, Nebraska, a rather serious mishap befell Quince Forrest, one of the men with the herd. He and the horse wrangler, who were bunkies, were constantly scuffling, reckless to the point of injury, the pulse of healthy manhood beating a constant alarm to rough contest.

The afternoon previous to the accident, a wayfaring man had overtaken the herd, and spent the night with the trail outfit. During the evening, a flock of sand-hill cranes was sighted, when the stranger expressed a wish to secure a specimen of the bird for its splendid plumage. On Forrest's own suggestion, his being a long-range pistol and the covey wary, the two exchanged belts. The visitor followed the flock, stealing within range a number of times, and emptying the six-shooter at every chance. On securing a fine specimen near nightfall, he returned to the herd, elated over his chance shot and beautiful trophy. However, before returning the belt, he had refilled the cylinder with six instead of five cartridges, thus resting the hammer on a loaded shell. In the enthusiasm of the moment, and ignorant of its danger, belt and pistol were returned to their owner.

Dawn found the camp astir. The sun had flooded the plain while the outfit was breakfasting, the herd was grazing forward in pastoral contentment, the horses stood under saddle for the morning's work, when the trail foreman, Paul Priest, languidly remarked: "If everybody's ready, we'll ride. Fill the canteens; it's high time we were in the saddle. Of course, that means the parting tussle between Quince and the wrangler. It would be a shame to deny those lads anything so enjoyable-- they remind me so much of mule colts and half-grown dogs. Now, cut in and worry each other a spell, because you'll be separated until noon. Fly at it, or we mount."

The two addressed never cast a glance at each other, but as the men swung into their saddles, the horse wrangler, with the agility of a tiger, caught his bunkie in the act of mounting, dragging him to the ground, when the expected scuffle ensued. The outfit had barely time to turn their horses, to witness the contest, when the two crashed against the wagon wheel and Forrest's pistol was discharged. The men dismounted instantly, the wrangler eased the victim to the ground, and when the outfit gathered around, the former was smothering the burning clothing of his friend and bunkmate. A withdrawn boot, dripping with blood, was the first indication of the havoc wrought, and on stripping it was found that the bullet had ploughed an open furrow down the thigh, penetrating the calf of the leg from knee to ankle, where it was fortunately deflected outward and into the ground.

The deepest of regret was naturally expressed. The jocular remarks of the foreman, the actions of the wrangler, were instantly recalled to the surrounding group, while the negligence which caused the accident was politely suppressed. The stranger, innocently unaware of any mistake on his part, lent a valuable hand in stanching the blood and in washing and binding up the wounds. No bones were injured, and with youth and a buoyant constitution, there was every hope of recovery.

However, some disposition must be made of the wounded man. No one could recall a house or settlement nearer than the Republican River, unless down the Beaver, which was uncertain, when the visitor came to the rescue. He was positive that some two years before, an old soldier had taken a homestead five or six miles above the trail crossing on the Beaver. He was insistent, and the foreman yielded so far as to order the herd grazed forward to the Beaver, which was some ten miles distant in their front. All the blankets in the outfit were accordingly brought into use, in making a comfortable bed in the wagon, and the caravan started, carrying the wounded man with it. Taking the stranger with him, the foreman bore away in the direction of the supposed homestead, having previously sent two men on an opposite angle, in search of any settlement down the creek.

The visitor's knowledge of the surrounding country proved to be correct. About six miles above the trail crossing, the Beaver, fringed with willows, meandered through a narrow valley, in which the homestead was located. The presence of the willows was an indication of old beaver dams, which the settler had improved until the water stood in long, placid pools. In response to their hail, two boys, about fourteen and sixteen years of age, emerged from the dug-out and greeted the horsemen. On inquiry, it proved that their father had died during the previous winter, at a settlement on the Solomon River, and the boys were then confronted with the necessity of leaving the claim to avoid suffering want. It was also learned that their mother had died before their father had taken the homestead, and therefore they were left orphans to fight their own battle.

The boys gave their names as Joel and Dell Wells. Both were bright-eyed and alert, freckled from the sun, ragged and healthy. Joel was the oldest, broad-shouldered for his years, distant by nature, with a shock of auburn hair, while Dell's was red; in height, the younger was the equal of his brother, talkative, and frank in countenance. When made acquainted with the errand of the trail boss, the older boy shook his head, but Dell stepped forward: "Awful sorry," said he, with a sweep of his hand, "but our garden failed, and there won't be a dozen roasting-ears in that field of corn. If hot winds don't kill it, it might make fodder. We expect to pull out next week."

"Have you no cows?" inquired the trail foreman.

"We had two, but the funeral expenses took them, and then pa's pension was stopped. You see--"

"I see," said the trail foreman, dismounting. "Possibly we can help each other. Our wagon is well provisioned. If you'll shelter and nurse this wounded man of mine--"

"We can't winter here," said Joel, stepping forward, "and the sooner we get out and find work the better."

"Oh, I was figuring on paying you wages," countered the trail man, now aware of their necessity, "and I suppose you could use a quarter of beef."

"Oh goodness," whispered Dell to his brother; "think, fresh meat."

"And I'll give each of you twenty-five dollars a month--leave the money with my man or pay you in advance. If you say the word, I'll unload my wagon right here, and grub-stake you for two months. I can get more provision at the Republican River, and in the mean time, something may turn up."

The stranger also dismounted and took part in urging the necessity of accepting the offer. Dell brightened at every suggestion, but his brother was tactful, questioning and combating the men, and looking well to the future. A cold and unfriendly world, coupled with misfortune, had aged the elder boy beyond his years, while the younger one was sympathetic, trustful, and dependent.

"Suppose we are delayed in reaching the Solomon until fall," said Dell to his brother; "that will put us into the settlements in time for corn-shucking. If you get six-bits a day, I'm surely worth fifty cents."

"Suppose there is no corn to shuck," replied Joel. "Suppose this wounded man dies on our hands? What then? Haven't you heard pa tell how soldiers died from slight wounds?--from blood-poisoning? If we have to go, we might as well go at once."

According to his light, the boy reasoned well. But when the wayfaring man had most skillfully retold the story of the Good Samaritan, the older boy relented somewhat, while Dell beamed with enthusiasm at the opportunity of rendering every assistance.

"It isn't because we don't want to help you," protested Joel, but it's because we're so poor and have nothing to offer."

"You have health and willing hands," said the trail boss; "let me do the rest."

"But suppose he doesn't recover as soon as expected," cautiously protested Joel, "where are we to get further provision?"

"Good suggestion," assented the trail foreman. "But here: I'll leave two good horses in your care for the wounded man, and all you need to do is to ride down to the trail, hail any passing herd, and simply tell them you are harboring a crippled lad, one of Don Lovell's boys, and you can levy on them for all they have. It's high time you were getting acquainted with these trail outfits. Shelter this man of mine, and all will come out well in the end. Besides, I'll tell old man Don about you boys, and he might take you home to his ranch with him. He has no boys, and he might take a fancy to you two."

Dell's eyes moistened at the suggestion of a home. The two brothers reëntered the dug-out, and the men led their horses down to the creek for a drink. A span of poor old mules stood inside a wooden corral, a rickety wagon and a few rusty farming implements were scattered about, while over all the homestead was the blight of a merciless summer drouth.

"What a pretty little ranch this would make," said the trail boss to the stranger. "If these boys had a hundred cows, with this water and range, in a few years they would be independent men. No wonder that oldest boy is cautious. Just look around and see the reward of their father's and their own labor. Their very home denies them bread."

"Did you notice the older boy brighten," inquired the visitor, "when you suggested leaving horses in their care? It was the only argument that touched him."

"Then I'll use it," said the trail boss, brightening. "We have several cow horses in our remuda, unfit for saddle,--galled backs and the like,-- and if these boys would care for them, I'll make their hungry hearts happy. Care and attention and a month's rest would make the ponies as sound as a dollar. You suggest my giving them each a saddle pony; argue the matter, and try and win me over."

The men retraced their steps, leading their horses, and when scarcely halfway from the creek to the dug-out, Dell ran down to meet them. "If you can spare us a few blankets and a pillow," earnestly said the boy, "we'll take the wounded man. He's liable to be feverish at night, and ought to have a pillow. Joel and I can sleep outside or in the stable."

"Hurrah for the Wells boys!" shouted the trail boss. "Hereafter I'll bet my money, horse and saddle, on a red-headed boy. Blankets? Why, you can have half a dozen, and as to pillows, watch me rob the outfit. I have a rubber one, there are several moss ones, and I have a lurking suspicion that there are a few genuine goose-hair pillows in the outfit, and you may pick and choose. They are all yours for the asking."

The men parleyed around some little time, offering pretexts for entering the shack, the interior of which bespoke its own poverty. When all agreements had been reviewed, the men mounted their horses, promising to fulfill their part of the covenant that afternoon or evening.

Once out of hearing, the stranger remarked: "That oldest boy is all right; it was their poverty that caused him to hesitate; he tried to shield their want. We men don't always understand boys. Hereafter, in dealing with Joel, you must use some diplomacy. The death of his parents has developed a responsibility in the older boy which the younger one doesn't feel. That's about all the difference in the two lads. You must deal gently with Joel, and never offend him or expose his needs."

"Trust me," replied the foreman, "and I'll coach Quince--that's the name of the wounded man. Within an hour, he'll be right at home with those boys. If nothing serious happens to his wound, within a week he'll have those youngsters walking on clouds."

The two men rode out of the valley, when they caught sight of a dust cloud, indicating the locality of the trailing herd, then hidden behind the last divide before reaching Beaver Creek. On every hand the undulating plain rolled away to low horizons, and the men rode forward at a leisurely pace.

"I've been thinking of those boys," suddenly said the trail foreman, arousing himself from a reverie. "They're to be pitied. This government ought to be indicted for running a gambling game, robbing children, orphan children of a soldier, at that. There's a fair sample of the skin game the government's running--bets you one hundred and sixty acres against fourteen dollars you can't hold down a homestead for five years. And big as the odds look, in nine cases out of ten, in this country, the government wins. It ought to be convicted on general principles. Men are not to be pitied, but it's a crime against women and children."

"Oh, you cowmen always rail at the settler," retorted the stranger; "you would kick if you were being hung. There's good in everything. A few years of youthful poverty, once they reach manhood, isn't going to hurt those boys. The school of experience has its advantages."

"If it's convenient, let's keep an eye on those boys the next few years," said the trail boss, catching sight of his remuda. "Now, there's the wagon. Suppose you ride down to the Beaver and select a good camp, well above the trail crossing, and I'll meet the commissary and herd. We'll have to lay over this afternoon, which will admit of watering the herd twice to-day. Try and find some shade."

The men separated, riding away on different angles. The foreman hailed his wagon, found the victim resting comfortably, and reported securing a haven for the wounded man. Instructing his cook to watch for a signal, at the hands of the stranger, indicating a camp on the creek, he turned and awaited the arrival of the lead cattle of the trailing column. Issuing orders to cover the situation, he called off half the men, first veering the herd to the nearest water, and rode to overtake his wagon and saddle horses.

Beaver Creek was barely running water, with an occasional long pool. A hedge of willows was interwoven, Indian fashion, from which a tarpaulin was stretched to the wagon bows, forming a sheltered canopy. Amid a fire of questions, the wounded man was lifted from the wagon.

"Are you sure there isn't a woman at this nester's shack," said he appealingly to the bearers of the blanket stretcher. "If there is, I ain't going. Paul, stand squarely in front of me, where I can see your eyes. After what I've been handed lately, it makes me peevish. I want to feel the walnut juice in your hand clasp. Now, tell it all over once more."

The stranger was artfully excused, to select a beef, after which the foreman sat down beside his man, giving him all the details and making valuable suggestions. He urged courteous treatment of their guest while he remained; that there was nothing to be gained, after the accident, by insult to a visitor, and concluded by praising the boys and bespeaking their protection.

The wounded man was Southern by birth and instinct, and knew that the hospitality of ranch and road and camp was one and the same. "Very well," said he, "but in this instance, remember it's my calf that's gored. Serves me right, though, kittening up to every stranger that comes along. I must be getting tired of you slatterly cow hands." He hesitated a moment. "The one thing I like," he continued, "about this nester layout is those red-headed boys. And these two are just about petting age. I can almost see them eating sugar out of my hand."

After dinner, and now that a haven was secured, the question of medical aid was considered. The couriers down the Beaver had returned and reported no habitation in that direction. Fortunately the destination of the stranger was a settlement on the Republican River, and he volunteered to ride through that afternoon and night and secure a surgeon. Frontier physicians were used to hundred-mile calls. The owner of the herd, had he been present, would have insisted on medical attention, the wounded man reluctantly consented, and the stranger, carrying a hastily written letter to Mr. Lovell, took his departure.

Early evening found the patient installed, not in the dug-out, but in a roomy tent. A quarter of beef hung on a willow, the one-room shack was bountifully provisioned, while the foreman remained to await the arrival of a physician. The day had brought forth wonders to Joel and Dell--from the dark hour of want to the dawn of plenty, while the future was a sealed book. In addition to the promised horses, Forrest's saddle hung in the sod stable, while two extra ponies aroused the wonder of the questioning boys.

"I just brought these two along," explained the foreman, "as their backs were galled during a recent rainy spell. You can see they are unfit for saddle, but with a little attention can be cured--I'll show you how. You have an abundance of water, and after I leave, wash their backs, morning and evening, and they'll be well in a month. Since you are running a trail hospital, you want to cater to man and beast. Of course, if you boys nurse this man through to health and strength, I'll make an appeal to Mr. Lovell to give you these ponies. They'll come in handy, in case you return to the Solomon, or start a little cattle ranch here."

The sun set in benediction on the little homestead. The transformation seemed magical. Even the blight of summer drouth was toned and tempered by the shadows of evening. The lesson of the day had filled empty hearts with happiness, and when darkness fell, the boys threw off all former reserve, and the bond of host and guest was firmly established. Forrest, even, cemented the tie, by dividing any needful attention between the boys.

"Do you know," said he to the foreman indifferently, in the presence of the lads, "that I was thinking of calling the oldest one Doc and the youngest one Nurse, but now I'm going to call them just plain Joel and Dell, and they can call me Mr. Quince. Honor bright, I never met a boy who can pour water on a wound, that seems to go to the right spot, like Dell Wells. One day with another, give me a red-headed boy."

CHAPTER II.
THE HOSPITAL ON THE BEAVER

The patient passed a feverish night. Priest remained on watch in the tent, but on several occasions aroused the boys, as recourse to pouring water was necessary to relieve the pain. The limb had reached a swollen condition by morning, and considerable anxiety was felt over the uncertainty of a physician arriving. If summoned the previous evening, it was possible that one might arrive by noon, otherwise there was no hope before evening or during the night.

"Better post a guide on the trail," suggested Joel. "If a doctor comes from the Republican, we can pilot him across the prairie and save an hour's time. There's a dim wagon trail runs from here to the first divide, north of the trail crossing on Beaver. Pa used it when he went to Culbertson to draw his pension. It would save the doctor a six or seven mile drive."

"Now, that suggestion is to the point," cheerfully assented the trail foreman. "The herd will noon on the first divide, and we can post the boys of the cut-off. They'll surely meet the doctor this afternoon or evening. Corral the horses, and I'll shorten up the stirrup straps on Forrest's saddle. Who will we send?"

"I'll go," said Dell, jumping at the opportunity. He had admired the horses and heavy Texas saddles the evening previous, and now that a chance presented itself, his eyes danced at the prospect. "Why, I can follow a dim wagon track," he added. "Joel and I used to go halfway to the divide, to meet pa when he bought us new boots."

"I'll see who can best be spared," replied Priest. "Your patient seems to think that no one can pour water like you. Besides, there will be plenty of riding to do, and you'll get your share."

The foreman delayed shortening the stirrup straps until after the horse stood saddled, when he adjusted the lacings as an object lesson to the boys. Both rode the same length of stirrup, mounting the horse to be fitted, and when reduced to the proper length, Dell was allowed to ride past the tent for inspection.

"There's the making of a born cowman," said Forrest, as Dell halted before the open tent. "It's an absolute mistake to think that that boy was ever intended for a farmer. Notice his saddle poise, will you, Paul? Has a pretty foot, too, even if it is slightly sun-burned. We must get him some boots. With that red hair, he never ought to ride any other horse than a black stallion."

When the question arose as to which of the boys was to be sent to intercept the moving herd and await the doctor, Forrest decided the matter. "I'll have to send Joel," said he, "because I simply can't spare Dell. The swelling has benumbed this old leg of mine, and we'll have to give it an occasional rubbing to keep the circulation up. There's where Dell has the true touch; actually he reminds me of my mother. She could tie a rag around a sore toe, in a way that would make a boy forget all his trouble. Hold Joel a minute."

The sound of a moving horse had caught the ear of the wounded man, and when the older boy dismounted at the tent opening, he continued: "Now, Joel, don't let that cow outfit get funny with you. Show them the brand on that horse you're riding, and give them distinctly to understand, even if you are barefooted, that you are one of Don Lovell's men. Of course you don't know him, but with that old man, it's love me, love my dog. Get your dinner with the outfit, and watch for a dust cloud in the south. There's liable to be another herd along any day, and we'll need a cow."

Forrest was nearly forty, while Priest was fully fifty years of age; neither had ever had children of his own, and their hearts went out in manly fullness to these waifs of the plain. On the other hand, a day had brought forth promise and fulfillment, from strangers, to the boys, until the latter's confidence knew no bounds. At random, the men virtually spoke of the cattle on a thousand hills, until the boys fully believed that by merely waving a wand, the bells would tinkle and a cow walk forth. Where two horses were promised, four had appeared. Where their little store of provision was as good as exhausted, it had been multiplied many fold. Where their living quarters were threatened with intrusion, a tent, with fly, was added; all of which, as if by magic, had risen out of a dip in the plain.

There was no danger, at the hands of the trail men, of any discourtesy to Joel, but to relieve any timidity, the foreman saddled his horse and accompanied the boy a mile or more, fully reviewing the details of his errand. Left behind, and while rubbing the wounded limb, Dell regaled his patient with a scrap of family history. "Pa never let us boys go near the trail," said he. "It seemed like he was afraid of you Texas men; afraid your cattle would trample down our fields and drink up all our water. The herds were so big."

"Suppose the cattle would drink the water," replied Forrest, "the owner would pay for it, which would be better than letting it go to waste. One day's hot winds would absorb more water than the biggest herd of cattle could drink. This ain't no farming country."

"That's so," admitted Dell; "we only had one mess of peas this season, and our potatoes aren't bigger than marbles. Now, let me rub your knee, there where the bullet skipped, between the bandages."

The rubbing over, Forrest pressed home the idea of abandoning farming for cattle ranching. "What your father ought to have done," said he, "was to have made friends with the Texas drovers; given them the water, with or without price, and bought any cripples or sore-footed cattle. Nearly every herd abandons more or less cattle on these long drives, and he could have bought them for a song and sung it himself. The buffalo grass on the divides and among these sand hills is the finest winter grazing in the country. This water that you are wasting would have yearly earned you one hundred head of cripples. A month's rest on this creek and they would kick up their heels and play like calves. After one winter on this range, they would get as fat as plover. Your father missed his chance by not making friends with the Texas trail men."

"Do you think so?" earnestly said Dell.

"I know it," emphatically asserted the wounded man. "Hereafter, you and Joel want to be friendly with these drovers and their men. Cast your bread upon the waters."

"Mother used to read that to us," frankly admitted Dell. There was a marked silence, only broken by a clatter of hoofs, and the trail boss cantered up to the tent.

"That wagon track," said he, dismounting, "is little more than a dim trail. Sorry I didn't think about it sooner, but we ought to have built a smudge fire where this road intersects the cattle trail. In case the doctor doesn't reach there by noon, I sent orders to fly a flag at the junction, and Joel to return home. But if the doctor doesn't reach there until after darkness, he'll never see the flag, and couldn't follow the trail if he did. We'll have to send Joel back."

"It's my turn," said Dell. "I know how to build a smudge fire; build it in a circle, out of cattle chips, in the middle of the road."

"You're a willing boy," said Priest, handing the bridle reins to Dell, "but we'll wait until Joel returns. You may water my horse and turn him in the corral."

The day wore on, and near the middle of the afternoon Joel came riding in. He had waited fully an hour after the departure of the herd, a flag had been left unfurled at the junction, and all other instructions delivered. Both Forrest and Priest knew the distance to the ford on the Republican, and could figure to an hour, by different saddle gaits, the necessary time to cover the distance, even to Culbertson. Still there was a measure of uncertainty: the messenger might have lost his way; there might not have been any physician within call; accidents might have happened to horse or rider,-- and one hour wore away, followed by another.

Against his will, Dell was held under restraint until six o'clock. "It's my intention to follow him within an hour," said the foreman, as the boy rounded a bluff and disappeared. "He can build the fire as well as any one, and we'll return before midnight. That'll give the doctor the last minute and the benefit of every doubt."

The foreman's mount stood saddled, and twilight had settled over the valley, when the occupants of the tent were startled by the neigh of a horse. "That's Rowdy," said Forrest; "he always nickers when he sights a wagon or camp. Dell's come."

Joel sprang to the open front. "It's Dell, and there's a buckboard following," he whispered. A moment later the vehicle rattled up, led by the irrepressible Dell, as if in charge of a battery of artillery. "This is the place, Doctor," said he, as if dismissing a troop from cavalry drill.

The physician proved to be a typical frontier doctor. He had left Culbertson that morning, was delayed in securing a relay team at the ford on the Republican, and still had traveled ninety miles since sunrise. "If it wasn't for six-shooters in this country," said he, as he entered the tent, "we doctors would have little to do. Your men with the herd told me how the accident happened." Then to Forrest, "Son, think it'll ever happen again?"

"Yes, unless you can cure a fool from lending his pistol," replied Forrest.

"Certainly. I've noticed that similarity in all gunshot wounds: they usually offer good excuses. It's healing in its nature," commented the doctor, as he began removing the bandages. As the examination proceeded, there was a running comment maintained, bordering on the humorous.

"If there's no extra charge," said Forrest, "I wish you would allow the boys to see the wounds. You might also deliver a short lecture on the danger of carrying the hammer of a pistol on a loaded cartridge. The boys are young and may take the lesson seriously, but you're wasting good breath on me. Call the boys--I'm an old dog."

"Gunshot wounds are the only crop in this country," continued the doctor, ignoring the request, "not affected by the drouth. There's an occasional outbreak of Texas fever among cattle, but that's not in my department. Well, that bullet surely was hungry for muscle, but fortunately it had a distaste for bone. This is just a simple case of treatment and avoiding complications. Six weeks to two months and you can buckle on your six-shooter again. Hereafter, better wear it on the other side, and if another accident occurs, it'll give you a hitch in each leg and level you up."

"But there may be no fool loafing around to borrow it," protested Forrest.

"Never fear, son; the fool's eternal," replied the doctor, with a quiet wink at the others.

The presence and unconcern of the old physician dispelled all uneasiness, and the night passed without anxiety, save between the boys. Forrest's lecture to Dell during the day, of the importance of making friends with the drovers, the value of the water, the purchase of disabled cattle, was all carefully reviewed after the boys were snugly in bed. "Were you afraid of the men with the herd to-day?--afraid of the cowboys?" inquired Dell, when the former subject was exhausted.

"Why, no," replied Joel rather scornfully, from the security of his bunk; "who would be afraid? They are just like any other folks."

Dell was skeptical. "Not like the pictures of cowboys?--not shooting and galloping their horses?"

"Why, you silly boy," said Joel, with contempt; "there wasn't a shot fired, their horses were never out of a walk, never wet a hair, and they changed to fresh ones at noon. The only difference I could see, they wore their hats at dinner. And they were surely cowboys, because they had over three thousand big beeves, and had come all the way from Texas."

"I wish I could have gone," was Dell's only comment.

"Oh, it was a great sight," continued the privileged one. "The column of cattle was a mile long, the trail twice as wide as a city street, and the cattle seemed to walk in loose marching order, of their own accord. Not a man carried a whip; no one even shouted; no one as much as looked at the cattle; the men rode away off yonder. The herd seemed so easy to handle."

"And how many men did it take?" insisted Dell.

"Only eleven with the herd. And they had such queer names for their places. Those in the lead were *point* men, those in the middle were *swing* men, and the one who brought up the rear was the *drag* man. Then there was the cook, who drove the wagon, and the wrangler, who took care of the horses--over one hundred and forty head. They call the band of saddle horses the remuda; one of the men told me it was Spanish for relay--a relay of horses."

"I'm going the next time," said Dell. "Mr. Quince said he would buy us a cow from the next herd that passed."

"These were all big beeves to-day, going to some fort on the Yellowstone River. And they had such wide, sweeping horns! And the smartest cattle! An hour before noon one of the point men gave a shrill whistle, and the whole column of beeves turned aside and began feeding. The men called it 'throwing the herd off the trail to graze.' It was just like saying *halt*! to soldiers--like we saw at that reunion in Ohio."

"And you weren't afraid?" timidly queried the younger brother.

"No one else was afraid, and why should I be? I was on horseback. Stop asking foolish questions and go to sleep," concluded Joel, with pitying finality, and turned to the wall.

"But suppose those big Texas beeves had stampeded, then what?" There was challenge in Dell's voice, but the brother vouchsafed no answer. A seniority of years had given one a twelve hours' insight over the other, in range cattle, and there was no common ground between sleepy bedfellows to justify further converse. "I piloted in the doctor, anyhow," said Dell defensively. No reply rewarded his assertion.

Morning brought little or no change in the condition of the wounds. The doctor was anxious to return, but Priest urged otherwise. "Let's call it Sunday," said he, "and not work to-day. Besides, if I overtake the herd, I'll have to make a hand. Wait until to-morrow, and we'll bear each other company. If another herd shows up on the trail to-day, it may have a cow. We must make these boys comfortable."

The doctor consented to stay over, and amused himself by quarreling with his patient. During the forenoon Priest and Joel rode out to the nearest high ground, from which a grove was seen on the upper Beaver. "That's what we call Hackberry Grove," said Joel, "and where we get our wood. The creek makes a big bend, and all the bottom land has grown up with timber, some as big as a man's body. It doesn't look very far away, but it takes all day to go and come, hauling wood. There's big springs just above, and the water never fails. That's what makes the trees so thrifty."

"Too bad your father didn't start a little ranch here," said Priest, surveying the scene. "It's a natural cattle range. There are the sand hills to the south; good winter shelter and a carpet of grass."

"We were too poor," frankly admitted the boy. "Every fall we had to go to the Solomon River to hunt work. With pa's pension, and what we could earn, we held down the homestead. Last fall we proved up; pa's service in the army counted on the residence required. It doesn't matter now if we do leave it. All Dell and I have to do is to keep the taxes paid."

"You would be doing wrong to leave this range," said the trail boss in fatherly tones. "There's a fortune in this grass, if you boys only had the cattle to eat it. Try and get a hundred cows on shares, or buy young steers on a credit."

"Why, we have no money, and no one would credit boys," ruefully replied Joel.

"You have something better than either credit or money," frankly replied the cowman; "you control this range. Make that the basis of your beginning. All these cattle that are coming over the trail are hunting a market or a new owner. Convince any man that you have the range, and the cattle will be forthcoming to occupy it."

"But we only hold a quarter-section of land," replied the boy in his bewilderment.

"Good. Take possession of the range, occupy it with cattle, and every one will respect your prior right," argued the practical man. "Range is being rapidly taken up in this western country. Here's your chance. Water and grass, world without end."

Joel was evidently embarrassed. Not that he questioned the older man's advice, but the means to the end seemed totally lacking. The grind of poverty had been his constant companion, until he scarcely looked forward to any reprieve, and the castles being built and the domain surveyed at the present moment were vague and misty. "I don't doubt your advice," admitted the boy. "A man could do it, you could, but Dell and I had better return to the settlements. Mr. Quince will surely be well by fall."

"Will you make me a promise?" frankly asked the cowman.

"I will," eagerly replied the boy.

"After I leave to-morrow morning, then, tell Forrest that you are thinking of claiming Beaver Creek as a cattle range. Ask him if he knows any way to secure a few cows and yearlings with which to stock it. In the mean time, think it over yourself. Will you do that?"

"Y-e-s, I--I will," admitted Joel, as if trapped into the promise.

"Of course you will. And ask him as if life and death depended on securing the cattle. Forrest has been a trail foreman and knows all the drovers and their men. He's liable to remain with you until the season ends. Now, don't fail to ask him."

"Oh, I'll ask him," said Joel more cheerfully. "Did you say that control of a range was a basis on which to start a ranch, and that it had a value?"

"That's it. Now you're catching the idea. Lay hold and never lose sight of the fact that a range that will graze five to ten thousand cattle, the year round, is as good as money in the bank."

Joel's faculties were grappling with the idea. The two turned their horses homeward, casting an occasional glance to the southward, but were unrewarded by the sight of a dust cloud, the signal of an approaching herd. The trail foreman was satisfied that he had instilled interest and inquiry into the boy's mind, which, if carefully nurtured, might result in independence. They had ridden several miles, discussing different matters, and when within sight of the homestead, Joel reined in his horse. "Would you mind repeating," said he, "what you said awhile ago, about control of a range by prior rights?"

The trail foreman freely responded to the awakened interest. "On the range," said he, "custom becomes law. No doubt but it dates back to the first flocks and herds. Its foundations rest on a sense of equity and justice which has always existed among pastoral people. In America it dates from the first invasion of the Spanish. Among us Texans, a man's range is respected equally with his home. By merely laying claim to the grazing privileges of public domain, and occupying it with flocks or herds, the consent of custom gives a man possession. It is an asset that is bought and sold, and is only lost when abandoned. In all human migrations, this custom has followed flocks and herds. Title to land is the only condition to which the custom yields."

"And we could claim this valley, by simply occupying it with cattle, and hold possession of its grazing privileges?" repeated the boy.

"By virtue of a custom, older than any law, you surely can. It's primal range to-day. This is your epoch. The buffalo preceded you, the settler, seeking a home, will follow you. The opportunity is yours. Go in and win."

"But how can we get a start of cattle?" pondered Joel.

"Well, after I leave, you're going to ask Forrest that question. That old boy knows all the ins and outs, and he may surprise you. There's an old maxim about where there's a will there's a way. Now if you have the will, I've a strong suspicion that your Mr. Quince will find the way. Try him, anyhow."

"Oh, I will," assured Joel; "the first thing in the morning."

The leaven of interest had found lodgment. A pleasant evening was spent in the tent. Before excusing the lads for the night, Priest said to the doctor: "This is a fine cattle range, and I'd like your opinion about these boys starting a little ranch on the Beaver."

"Well," said the old physician, looking from Joel to Dell, "there are too many lawyers and doctors already. The farmers raise nothing out here, and about the only prosperous people I meet are you cowmen. You ride good horses, have means to secure your needs, and your general health is actually discouraging to my profession. Yes, I think I'll have to approve of the suggestion. A life in the open, an evening by a camp-fire, a saddle for a pillow--well, I wish I had my life to live over. It wouldn't surprise me to hear of Wells Brothers making a big success as ranchmen. They have health and youth, and there's nothing like beginning at the bottom of the ladder. In fact, the proposition has my hearty approval. Fight it out, boys; start a ranch."

"Come on, Dell," said Joel, leading the way; "these gentlemen want to make an early start. You'll have to bring in the horses while I get breakfast. Come on."

CHAPTER III.
THE BOTTOM RUNG

An early start was delayed. Joel had figured without his guest, as the Texan stands in a class by himself. The peace and serenity of pastoral life affects its people, influencing their normal natures into calm and tranquil ways. Hence, instead of the expected start at sunrise, after breakfast the trail foreman languidly sauntered out to the corral, followed by the boys.

The old physician, even, grew impatient. "What on earth do you think is detaining that man?" he inquired of Forrest. "Here the sun is nearly an hour high, and not a wheel turning. And I can see him from the tent opening, sitting on a log, flicking the ground with his quirt and chatting with those boys. What do you suppose they are talking about?"

"Well, now, that's a hard question," answered Forrest. "I'll chance the subject is of no importance. Just a little social powwow with the boys, most likely. Sit down, Doctor, and take life easy--the cows will calve in the spring."

Patience had almost ceased to be a virtue when the trail boss put in an appearance at the tent. "You are in no particular hurry, are you, Doctor?" he inquired, with a friendly smile.

"Oh, no," said the physician, with delightful irony; "I was just thinking of having the team unhooked, and lay over another day. Still, I am some little distance from home, and have a family that likes to see me occasionally."

The buckboard rattled away. "Come in the tent," called Forrest to the boys. "If old Paul sees you standing out there, he's liable to think of something and come back. Honestly, when it comes to killing time, that old boy is the bell steer."

Only three were now left at the homestead. The first concern was to intercept the next passing herd. Forrest had a wide acquaintance among trail foremen, had met many of them at Dodge only ten days before, while passing that supply point, and it was a matter of waiting until a herd should appear.

There was little delay. Joel was sent at ten o'clock to the nearest swell, and Dell an hour later. The magic was working overtime; the dust cloud was there! In his haste to deliver the message, the sentinel's horse tore past the tent and was only halted at the corral. "It's there!" he shouted, returning, peering through the tent-flaps. "They're coming; another herd's coming. It's in the dip behind the first divide. Shall I go? I saw it first."

"Dismount and rest your saddle," said Forrest. "Come in and let's make a little medicine. If this herd has one, here's where we get a cow. Come in and we'll plot against the Texans."

With great misgiving, Dell dismounted. As he entered the tent, Forrest continued: "Sit on the corner of my bunk, and we'll talk the situation over. Oh, I'm going to send you, never fear. Now, the trouble is, we don't know whose herd this may be, and you must play innocent and foxy. If the herd is behind the first divide, it'll water in the Beaver about four o'clock. Now, ride down the creek and keep your eagle eye open for a lone horseman, either at the crossing or on the trail. That's the foreman, and that's the man we want to see. He may be ten miles in the lead of his herd, and you want to ride straight to him. Give him all the information you can regarding the water, and inquire if this is one of Lovell's herds. That will put you on a chatting basis, and then lead up to your errand. Tell him that you are running a trail hospital, and that you have a wounded man named Quince Forrest at your camp, and ask the foreman to come up and see him. Once you get him here, your work is over, except going back after the cow."

Dell was impatient to be off, and started for the opening. "Hold on," commanded Forrest, "or I'll put a rope on you. Now, ride slowly, let your horse set his own pace, and don't come back without your man. Make out that I'm badly wounded, and that you feel uneasy that blood poisoning may set in."

The messenger lost no time in getting away. Once out of sight of the tent, Dell could not resist the temptation to gallop his mount over level places. Carrying the weight of a boy was nothing to the horse, and before half an hour had passed, the ford and trail came in view of the anxious courier. Halting in order to survey the horizon, the haze and heat-waves of summer so obstructed his view that every object looked blurred and indistinct. Even the dust cloud was missing; and pushing on a mile farther, he reined in again. Now and then in the upper sky, an intervening cloud threw a shadow over the plain, revealing objects more distinctly. For a moment one rested over the trail crossing, and like prophecy fulfilled, there was the lone horseman at the ford!

In the waste places it is a pleasure to unexpectedly meet a fellow being. Before being observed, Dell rode within hailing distance, greeting, and man and boy were soon in friendly converse. There was water sufficient for all needs, the herd required no pilot, the summons found a ready response, and the two were soon riding up the Beaver in a jog trot.

The gait admitted of free conversation, and the new foreman soon had Dell on the defensive. "I always hate to follow a Lovell outfit," said the stranger regretfully; "they're always in trouble. Old man Don's a nice enough man, but he sure works sorry outfits on the trail. I've been expecting to hear something like this. If it isn't rebranding their saddle stock with nigger brands, it's sure to be something worse. And now that flat-headed Quince Forrest plows a fire-guard down his own leg with a six-shooter! Well, wouldn't that sour sweet milk!"

"Oh, it wasn't his fault," protested Dell; "he only loaned his pistol, and it was returned with the hammer on a cartridge."

"Of course," disgustedly assented the trail boss; "with me it's an old story. Hadn't no more sabe than to lend his gun to some prowling tenderfoot. More than likely he urged its loan on this short-horn. Yes, I know Colonel Forrest; I've known him to bet his saddle and ride bareback as the result. It shows his cow-sense. Rather shallow-brained to be allowed so far from home."

"Well," contended poor Dell, "they surely were no friends. At least Mr. Quince don't speak very highly of that man."

"That's his hindsight," said the trail foreman. "If the truth ever comes out, you'll notice his foresight was different. Colonel Quince is famous, after the horse is stolen, for locking the stable door. That other time he offered to take an oath, on a stack of Bibles, never to bet his saddle again. The trouble is the game never repeats; the play never comes up twice alike. If that old boy's gray matter ever comes to full bloom, long before his allotted time, he'll wither away."

Dell was discouraged. He realized that his defense of his friend was weak. This second foreman seemed so different from either Priest or Forrest. He spoke with such deep regret of the seeming faults of others that the boy never doubted his sincerity. He even questioned Dell with such an innocent countenance that the lad withered before his glance, and became disheartened at the success of the errand. Forced to the defense continually, on several occasions Dell nearly betrayed the object of bringing the new man to the homestead, but in each instance was saved by some fortunate turn in the conversation. Never was sight more welcome than the tent, glistening in the sun, and never was relief from duty more welcome to a courier. The only crumb of comfort left to the boy who had ridden forth so boldly was that he had not betrayed the object of his mission and had brought the range men together. Otherwise his banner was trailing in the dust.

The two rode direct to the tent. During the middle of the day, in order to provide free ventilation, the walls were tucked up, and the flaps, rear and front, thrown wide open. Stretched on his bunk, Forrest watched the opening, and when darkened by the new arrival, the wounded man's greeting was most cordial. "Well, if it isn't old Nat Straw," said he, extending his hand. "Here, I've been running over in my mind the different trail bosses who generally go north of the Platte River, but you escaped my memory. It must have gotten into my mind, somehow, that you had married and gone back to chopping cotton. Still driving for Uncle Jess Ellison, I reckon?"

"Yes, still clerking for the same drover," admitted Straw, glancing at the wounded limb. "What's this I hear about you laying off, and trying to eat some poor nester out of house and home? You must be getting doty."

"Enjoy yourself, Nat. The laugh's on me. I'm getting discouraged that I'll ever have common horse sense. Isn't it a shame to be a fool all your life!"

Straw glanced from the bunk to Dell. "I was just telling the boy, as we rode up the creek, that you needed a whole heap of fixing in your upper loft. The poor boy tried his best to defend you, but it was easy to see that he hadn't known you long."

"And of course you strung him for all he could carry," said Forrest. "Here, Dell. You were in such a hurry to get away that I overlooked warning you against these trail varmints. Right now, I can see old Nat leading you in under a wet blanket, and your colors dragging. Don't believe a word he told you, and don't even give him a pleasant look while he stays here."

The discouraged boy brightened, and Joel and Dell were excused, to water and picket the horses. "You ought to be ashamed of yourself," resumed Forrest, "brow-beating that boy. Considering my hard luck, I've fallen into angels' hands. These boys are darling fellows. Now before you leave, square yourself with that youngest one."

"A little jollying while he's young won't hurt him," replied Straw. "It's not a bad idea to learn early to believe nothing that you hear and only half of what you see. If you had been taken snipe hunting oftener when you were young, it wouldn't hurt you any now. There are just about so many knocks coming to each of us, and we've got to take them along with the croup, chicken-pox, measles, and mumps."

During the absence of the boys, Forrest informed Straw of the sad condition which confronted the lads, when accident and necessity threw him into their hands. He also repeated Priest's opinion of the valuable range, unoccupied above on the Beaver, and urged his assistance in securing some cattle with which to stock and claim it for the boys.

"There's plenty of flotsam on the trail," said he, "strays and sore-footed cattle, to occupy this valley and give these boys a start in life. I never even got thanked for a stray, and I've turned hundreds of them loose on these upper ranges, refused on the delivery of a herd. Somebody gets them, and I want these boys of mine to get a few hundred head during this summer. Here's the place to drop your cripples and stray cows. From what Paul says, there's range above here for thousands of cattle, and that's the foundation of a ranch. Without a hoof on it, it has a value in proportion to its carrying capacity, and Priest and I want these boys to secure it. They've treated me white, and I'm going to make a fight for them."

The appeal was not in vain. "Why not," commented Straw. "Let me in and we'll make it three-handed. My herd is contracted again this year to the same cattle company on the Crazy Woman, in Wyoming, as last season, and I want to fool them this trip. They got gay on my hands last summer, held me down to the straight road brand at delivery, and I'll see to it that there are no strays in my herd this year. I went hungry for fresh beef, and gave those sharks over forty good strays. They knew I'd have to leave them behind me. Watch me do it again."

"About how many have you now, and how do they run?"

"They're a hit-and-miss lot, like strays always are. Run from a good cow down to yearlings. There ought to be about twenty-five head, and I'll cut you out five or six cripples. They could never make it through, nohow."

"Any calves among the strays?"

"Two or three."

"Good enough. Give each of the boys a cow and calf, and the others to me. We'll let on that I've bought them."

That no time might be lost in friendly chat, a late dinner was eaten in the tent. Straw would have to meet his herd at the trail crossing that afternoon, which would afford an opportunity to cut out all strays and cripples. One of the boys would return with him, for the expected cow, and when volunteers were called for, Dell hesitated in offering his services. "I'll excuse you," said Straw to Joel, who had jumped at the chance. "I'm a little weak on this redheaded boy, and when a cow hand picks on me for his side partner, the choice holds until further orders. Bring in the horses off picket, son, and we'll be riding."

The latter order was addressed to Dell. No sooner had the boy departed than Straw turned to Joel. "I've fallen head over ears in love with the idea of this trail hospital. Just where it ought to be; just about midway between Dodge and Ogalalla. Of course I'm hog wild to get in on it. I might get a man hurt any day, might get sick myself, and I want to be a stockholder in this hospital of yours. What's your favorite color in cows?"

Joel's caution caused him to hesitate. "If you have one, send me a milk-white cow *with a black face*" instantly said Forrest. "White cows are rich in cream, and I'm getting peevish, having to drink black coffee."

"A white cow for you," said Straw, nodding to Forrest, "and what color for you?" But Joel, although half convinced, made no answer.

"Send him a red one," authorized Forrest; "red steers bring a dollar a head more than mongrel colors."

"A red cow and calf for Joel, a white one for milk, and Dell can pick his own," said Straw, murmuring a memorandum. "Now, that little passel of cripples, and odds and ends," again nodding to Forrest, "that I'm sawing off on you, I'll bring them up with the cows. Yes, I'm coming back and stay all night."

Joel lost all doubts on the moment. The trail boss was coming back, was going to bring each one a cow. There was no question but that this stranger had the cattle in his possession; surely he would not trifle with his own people, with an unfortunate, wounded man. All this seemed so in keeping with the partial outline of Priest, the old gray-haired foreman, that the boy's caution gave place to firm belief. If generous princes ever walked the earth, it was just possible that liberal ones in the rough were still riding it in disguise.

Joel hastened to his brother with the news. "It's all right," said he, throwing the saddle on Straw's horse. "You go right along with this strange foreman. He gave Mr. Quince a milk cow, a white one, and you're to pick one for yourself. If I were going in your place, I'd pick a red one; red cattle are worth a dollar a head more than any other color."

There was something in Joel's voice that told Dell that his brother had not been forgotten. "And you?--don't you?" stammered the younger boy.

"Mr. Quince picked out a cow and calf for me," replied Joel, with a loftiness that two years' seniority confers on healthy boys. "I left it to him to choose mine. You'd better pick out a red one. And say, this hospital of ours is the real thing. It's the only one between Dodge and Ogalalla. This strange foreman wants to take stock in it. I wonder if that was what he meant by sawing off a little passel of cattle on Mr. Quince. Now, don't argue or ask foolish questions, but keep your eyes and ears open."

Fortified anew in courage, Dell accompanied the trail boss to meet his herd. It was a short hour's ride, and on sighting the cattle, then nearing the crossing, they gave rein to their horses and rode for the rear of the long column, where, in the rear-guard of the trailing cattle, naturally the sore and tender-footed animals were to be found. The drag men knew them to a hoof, were delighted to hear that all cripples were to be dropped, and half a dozen were cut off and started up the Beaver. "Nurse them to the nearest water," said Straw to the drag men, "and then push them up the creek until I overtake you. Here's where we drop our strays and cripples. What? No, I'm only endowing a trail hospital."

The herd numbered thirty-one hundred two-year-old steers. They filled the channel of the Beaver for a mile around the crossing, crowding into the deeper pools, and thrashing up and down the creek in slaking their thirst. Dell had never seen so many cattle, almost as uniform in size as that many marbles, and the ease with which a few men handled the herd became a nine-day wonder to the astonished boy. And when the word passed around to cut all strays up the creek, the facility with which the men culled out the alien down to one class and road brand, proved them masters in the craft. It seemed as easily done as selecting a knife from among the other trinkets in a boy's pocket.

After a change of mounts for the foreman, Dell and the trail boss drifted the strays up the creek. The latter had counted and classed them as cut out of the herd, and when thrown together with the cripples, the promised little passel numbered thirty-five cattle, not counting three calves. Straw excused his men, promising to overtake them the next morning, and man and boy drifted the nucleus of a future ranch toward the homestead.

"Barring that white cow and the red one with the speckled calf," said Straw to Dell, pointing out each, "you're entitled to pick one for yourself. Now, I'm not going to hurry you in making your choice. Any time before we sight the tent and shack, you are to pick one for your own dear cow, and stand by your choice, good or bad. Remember, it carries my compliments to you, as one of the founders of the first hospital on the Texas and Montana cattle trail."

Two miles below the homestead, the half-dozen cripples were dropped to the rear. "You can come back to-morrow morning and get these tender steers," said the foreman, "and drift them up above the improvements. You'll find them near here on the water. Now, we'll sight the tent around the next bend, and you may point out your choice."

"I'll take that red steer," said Dell with marked decision, pointing out a yearling.

A peal of laughter greeted his choice. "That's a boy," shouted Straw; "shoot at a buck and kill a fawn! Why didn't you take that black cow and calf?"

"I like red cattle the best," replied Dell, undaunted. "I've heard they bring a better price. I'll own the only red steer in the bunch."

"Yes, but when your choice is a beef, that black cow and her increase would buy two beeves. Dell, if you ever get to be a cowman, you'll have to do some of your own thinking."

Dell's mistake was in listening to others. Joel was equally guilty, as his lofty comments regarding red cattle were derived from the random remarks of Forrest. The brothers were novices in range cattle, and Dell's error was based in not relying on his own judgment.

On sighting the approaching cattle, Forrest's bunk was eased around to the tent opening, Joel holding the flaps apart, and the little herd was grazed past at a snail's pace in review. Leaving Dell to nurse the nucleus past the improvements, Straw dismounted at the tent. "Well," said he, handing the bridle reins to Joel, "that red-headed Dell is surely the making of a great cowman. All successful men begin at the bottom of the ladder, and he surely put his foot on the lowest rung. What do you suppose his choice was?"

"The bottom rung suggests a yearling," said Forrest.

"Stand up. You spelled the word correct. I'm a sheep herder, if he didn't pick out the only, little, old, red, dobe steer in the entire bunch!"

Forrest eased himself down on the bunk, unable to restrain his laughter. "Well," said he, "we all have to learn, and no one can say Dell wasn't true to his colors."

CHAPTER IV.
THE BROTHERS CLAIM A RANGE

The next morning Straw dallied about until Dell brought up the crippled cattle. They were uniform in size; rest was the one thing needful, and it now would be theirs amid bountiful surroundings. They were driven up among the others, now scattered about in plain sight in the valley above, presenting a morning scene of pastoral contentment.

"Even the calves are playing this morning," said Straw to Forrest, as the former entered the tent. "A few cattle surely make this valley look good. What you want to do now is to keep on drawing more. Don't allow no outfit to pass without chipping in, at least give them the chance, and this trail hospital will be on velvet in no time. Of course, all Lovell outfits will tear their shirts boosting the endowment fund, but that needn't bar the other herds. Some outfits may have no cattle, but they can chip in a sore-back or crippled pony. My idea is to bar no one, and if they won't come in, give them a chance to say they don't want to. You ought to send word back to Dodge; any foreman going east or west from there would give you his strays."

The conception of a trail refuge had taken root. The supply points were oases for amusement, but a halfway haven for the long stretches of unsettled country, during the exodus of Texas cattle to the Northwest, was an unknown port. The monotony of from three to five months on the trail, night and day work, was tiring to men, while a glass of milk or even an hour in the shade was a distinct relief. Straw was reluctant to go, returning to make suggestions, by way of excuse, and not until forced by the advancing day did he mount and leave to overtake his herd.

Again the trio was left alone. Straw had given Forrest a list of brands and a classification of the cattle contributed, and a lesson in reading brands was given the boys. "Brands read from left to right," said Forrest to the pair of attentive listeners, "or downward. If more than one brand is on an animal, the upper one is the holding or one in which ownership is vested. Character brands are known by name, and are used because difficult to alter. There is scarcely a letter in the alphabet that a cattle thief can't change. When a cow brute leaves its home range, it's always a temptation to some rustler to alter the brand, and characters are not so easily changed."

The importance of claiming the range was pressing, and now that cattle were occupying it, the opportunity presented itself. A notice was accordingly written, laying claim to all grazing rights, from the Texas and Montana trail crossing on Beaver to the headwaters of the same, including all its tributaries, by virtue of possession and occupancy vested in the claimants, Wells Brothers. "How does that sound?" inquired Forrest, its author, giving a literal reading of the notice. "Nothing small or stingy about that, eh? When you're getting, get a-plenty."

"But where are we to get the cattle to stock such a big country?" pondered Joel. "It's twenty miles to the head of this creek."

"We might as well lay big plans as little ones. Here's where we make a spoon or spoil a horn. Saddle a horse and post this notice down at the trail crossing. Sink a stake where every one can see it, and nail your colors to the sign-board. We are the people, and must be respected."

Joel hastened away to post the important notice. Dell was detailed on sentinel duty, on lookout for another herd, but each trip he managed to find some excuse to ride among the cattle. "What's the brand on my white cow?" inquired Forrest, the object leading up to another peculiarity in color.

"I couldn't *read* it," said Dell, airing his range parlance.

"No? Well, did you ever see a white cow with a black face?" inquired the wounded man, coming direct to the matter at issue.

"Not that I remember; why?"

"Because there never lived such a colored cow. Nature has one color that she never mars. You can find any colored cow with a white face, but you'll never find a milk-white cow with a colored face. That line is drawn, and you want to remember it. You'll never shoot a wild swan with a blue wing, or see yellow snowflakes fall, or meet a pure white cow with a black face. Hereafter, if any one attempts to send you on a wild-goose chase, to hunt such a cow, tell them that no such animal ever walked this earth."

Joel returned before noon. No sign of an approaching herd was sighted by the middle of the afternoon, and the trio resigned themselves to random conversation.

"Dell," said Forrest, "it's been on my mind all day to ask you why you picked a yearling yesterday when you had a chance to take a cow. Straw laughed at you."

"Because Joel said red cattle were worth a dollar a head more than any other color."

"Young man," inquired Forrest of Joel, "what's your authority for that statement?"

"Didn't you pick me a red cow yesterday, and didn't you admit to Mr. Straw that red cattle were worth the most?" said Joel, in defense of his actions.

"And you rushed away and palmed my random talking off on Dell as original advice? You'll do. Claiming a little more than you actually know will never hurt you any. Now here's a prize for the best brand reader: The boy who brings me a correct list of brands, as furnished by Straw, gets my white cow and calf as a reward. I want the road and ranch brand on the cripples, and the only or holding brand on the others. Now, fool one another if you can. Ride through them slowly, and the one who brings me a perfect list is my bully boy."

The incentive of reward stimulated the brothers to action. They scampered away on ponies, not even waiting to saddle, and several hours were spent in copying brands. These included characters, figures, and letters, and to read them with skill was largely a matter of practice. Any novice ought to copy brands, but in this instance the amateur's list would be compared with that of an experienced trail foreman, a neutral judge from which there was no appeal.

The task occupied the entire evening. Forrest not only had them read, but looked over each copy, lending impartial assistance in reading characters that might baffle a boy. There were some half dozen of the latter in Straw's list, a *turkey track* being the most difficult to interpret, but when all characters were fully understood, Joel still had four errors to Dell's three. The cripples were found to be correct in each instance, and were exempt from further disturbance. Forrest now insisted that to classify, by enumerating each grade, would assist in locating the errors, which work would have to be postponed until morning.

The boys were thoroughly in earnest in mastering the task. Forrest regaled them with examples of the wonderful expertness of the Texans in reading brands and classifying cattle. "Down home," said he, "we have boys who read brands as easily as a girl reads a novel. I know men who can count one hundred head of mixed cattle, as they leave a corral, or trail along, and not only classify them but also give you every brand correctly. Now, that's the kind of cowmen I aim to make out of you boys, and to-morrow morning you must get these brands accurate. What was that?"

Both boys sprang to the tent opening and listened. It sounded like a shot, and within a few moments was seconded by a distant hail.

"Some one must be lost," suggested Joel. "He's down the creek."

"Lost your grandmother!" exclaimed Forrest. "We're all lost in this country. Here, fire this six-shooter in the air, and follow it up with a Comanche yell. Dell, build a little fire on the nearest knoll. It's more than likely some trail man hunting this camp."

The signal-fire was soon burning. The only answer vouchsafed was some fifteen minutes later, when the clatter of an approaching horse was distinctly heard. A lantern shone through the tent walls, and the prompt hail of the horseman proved him no stranger. "Is Quince Forrest here?" he inquired, as his horse shied at the tent.

"He is. Come in, Dorg," said Forrest, recognizing by his voice the horseman without to be Dorg Seay, one of Don Lovell's foremen. "Come in and let us feast our eyes on your handsome face."

Seay peeped within and timidly entered. "Well," said he, pulling at a straggling mustache, "evidently it isn't as bad as reported. Priest wrote back to old man Don that you had attempted suicide--unfortunate in love was the reason given--and I have orders to inquire into your health or scatter flowers on your grave. Able to sit up and take notice?--no complications, I hope?"

"When did you leave Dodge?" inquired Forrest, ignoring Seay's persiflage.

"About a week ago. A telegram was waiting me on the railroad, and I rode through this afternoon. If this ranch boasts anything to eat, now would be an awful nice time to mention it."

Seay's wants were looked after.

"How many herds between here and the railroad?" inquired Forrest, resuming the conversation.

"Only one ahead of mine. In fact, I'm foreman of both herds--live with the lead one and occasionally go back and see my own. It all depends on who feeds best."

"And when will your herd reach the Beaver?" continued Forrest.

"I left orders to water my lead herd in the Beaver at three o'clock to-morrow, and my own dear cattle will be at their heels. My outfit acts as rear-guard to Blocker's herd."

These men, in the employ of the same drover, had not seen each other in months, and a fire of questions followed, and were answered. The chronicle of the long drive, of accident by flood and field, led up to the prospects for a northern demand for cattle.

"The market has barely opened in Dodge," said Seay, in reply to a question. "Unless the herds are sold or contracted, very few will leave Dodge for the Platte River before the first of July. Old man Don isn't driving a hoof that isn't placed, so all his herds will pass Ogalalla before the first of the month. The bulk of the drive going north of the Platte will come next month. With the exception of scattering herds, the first of August will end the drive."

The men talked far into the night. When they were left alone in the tent, Forrest unfolded his plans for starting the boys in life.

"We found them actually on their uppers," said he; "they hadn't tasted meat in months, and were living on greens and garden truck. It's a good range, and we must get them some cattle. The first year may be a little tough, but by drawing on all of Lovell's wagons for the necessary staples, we can provision them until next spring. You must leave some flour and salt and beans and the like."

"Beans!" echoed Seay. "That will surely tickle my cook. Did you ever notice that the farther north it goes, a Texas trail outfit gets tastier? Let it start out on bacon and beans and blackstrap, and after the herd crosses the Platte, the varmints want prairie chicken and fried trout. Tasty! Why, those old boys develop an elegant taste for dainties. Nothing but good old beef ever makes them even think of home again. Yes, my cook will give you his last bean, and make a presentation speech gratis."

Forrest's wound had begun to mend, the soreness and swelling had left the knee joint, and the following morning Seay spent in making crutches. Crude and for temporary use, the wounded man tried them out, and by assistance reached the entrance, where he was eased into an old family rocking-chair in the shade of the tent.

"This has been the dream of my life," said he, "to sit like some old patriarch in my tent door and count my cattle. See that white cow yonder?" pointing with a crutch. "Well, she belongs to your uncle John Quincy. And that reminds me that she and her calf are up as a reward to complete the roll of brands. Boys, are you ready?"

The revised lists were submitted for inspection. Compared with the one rendered by Straw, there was still a difference in Dell's regarding a dun cow, while Joel's list varied on three head. Under the classification the errors were easily located, and summoning the visiting foreman, Forrest explained the situation.

"I'll have to appoint you umpire in deciding this matter. Here's the roll furnished by Nat Straw, and you'll compare it with Dell and Joel's. Of course, old Nat didn't care a whoopee about getting the list perfect, and my boy may be right on that dun cow. Joel differs on a three-year-old, a heifer, and a yearling steer. Now, get them straight, because we're expecting to receive more cattle this evening. Pass on these brands before you leave to meet your herd this afternoon. And remember, there's a cow and calf at stake for whichever one of these boys first gets the roll correct."

After dinner the three rode away for a final inspection. The cattle were lazy and logy from water, often admitting of riding within a rod, thus rendering the brands readable at a glance. Dell led the way to the dun cow, but before Seay could pass an opinion, the boy called for his list in possession of the man. "Let me take my roll a minute," said he, "and I'll make the correction. It isn't a four bar four, it's four equals four; there's two bars instead of one. The cow and calf is mine. That gives me three."

The lust of possession was in Dell's voice. The reward had been fairly earned, and turning to the other cattle in dispute, Joel's errors were easily corrected. All three were in one brand, and the mere failure to note the lines of difference between the figure eight and the letter S had resulted in repeating the mistake. Seay amused himself by pointing out different animals and calling for their brands, and an envious rivalry resulted between the brothers, in their ability to read range script.

"A good eye and a good memory," said Seay, as they rode homeward, "are gifts to a cowman. A brand once seen is hardly ever forgotten. Twenty years hence, you boys will remember all these brands. One man can read brands at twice the distance of another, and I have seen many who could distinguish cattle from horses, with the naked eye, at a distance of three miles. When a man learns to know all there is about cattle, he ought to be getting gray around the edges."

Forrest accepted the umpire's report. "I thought some novice might trip his toe on that equality sign," said he. "There's nothing like having studied your arithmetic. Dell's been to school, and it won him a cow and calf when he saw the sign used as a brand. I wonder how he is on driving mules."

"I can drive them," came the prompt reply.

"Very well. Hook up the old team. I'm sending you down to the trail crossing to levy on two commissary wagons. Take everything they give you and throw out a few hints for more. This afternoon we begin laying in a year's provisions. It may be a cold winter, followed by a late spring, and there's nothing like having enough. Relieve them of all their dried fruits, and make a strong talk for the staples of life. I may want to winter here myself, and a cow camp should make provision for more or less company."

Seay lent his approval. "Hitch up and rattle along ahead of me," said he. "The wagons may reach the crossing an hour or two ahead of the herds, and I'll be there to help you trim them down to light traveling form."

It proved an active afternoon. The wagon was started for the trail crossing, followed by Seay within half an hour. Joel was in a quandary, between duty and desire, as he was anxious to see the passing herds, yet a bond of obligation to the wounded man required his obedience. Forrest had noticed the horse under saddle, the impatience of the boy, but tactfully removed all uneasiness.

"I have been trying to figure out," said he, "how I could spare you this afternoon, as no doubt you would like to see the herds, but we have so much to do at home. Now that I can hobble out, you must get me four poles, and we will strip this fly off the tent and make a sunshade out of it--make an arbor in front of our quarters. Have the props ready, and in the morning Seay will show you how to stretch a tarpaulin for a sunshade. And then along towards evening, you must drift our little bunch of cattle at least a mile up the creek. I'm expecting more this evening, and until we learn the brands on this second contingent, they must be kept separate. And then, since we've claimed it, we want to make a showing of occupying the range, by scattering the cattle over it. Within a month, our cows must rest in the shade of Hackberry Grove and be watering out of those upper springs. When you take a country, the next thing is to hold it."

Something to do was a relief to Joel. Willow stays, for the arbor, were cut, the bark peeled off, and the poles laid ready at hand. When the cattle arose, of their own accord, from the noonday rest, the impatient lad was allowed to graze them around the bend of the creek. There was hardly enough work to keep an active boy employed, and a social hour ensued. "Things are coming our way," said Forrest. "This man Seay will just about rob Blocker's outfit. When it comes to making a poor mouth, that boy Dorg is in a class by himself. Dell will just about have a wagon load. You boys will have to sleep in the tent hereafter."

It proved so. The team returned an hour before sunset, loaded to the carrying capacity of the wagon. Not only were there remnants in the staples of life, but kegs of molasses and bags of flour and beans, while a good saddle, coils of rope, and a pair of new boots which, after a wetting, had proven too small for the owner, were among the assets. It was a motley assortment of odds and ends, a free discard of two trail outfits, all of which found an acceptable lodgment at the new ranch.

"They're coming up to supper," announced Dell to Forrest. "Mr. Blocker's foreman knows you, and sent word to get up a spread. He says that when he goes visiting, he expects his friends to not only put on the little and big pot, but kill a chicken and churn. He's such a funny fellow. He made me try on those boots, and when he saw they would fit, he ordered their owner, one of Mr. Seay's men, to give them to me or he would fight him at sunrise."

"Had them robbing each other for us, eh?" said Forrest, smiling. "Well, that's the kind of friend to have when settling up a new country. This ranch is like a fairy story. Here I sit and wave my crutch for a wand, and everything we need seems to just bob up out of the plain. Cattle coming along to stock a ranch, old chum coming to supper, in fact, everything coming our way. Dell, get up a banquet--who cares for expense!"

It was barely dusk when the second contingent of cattle passed above the homestead and were turned loose for the night. As before, the cripples had been dropped midway, and would be nursed up the next morning. With the assistance of crutches, Forrest managed to reach the opening, and by clinging to the tent-pole, waved a welcome to the approaching trail men.

Blocker's foreman, disdaining an invitation to dismount, saluted his host. "There's some question in my mind," said he, "as to what kind of a dead-fall you're running up here, but if it's on the square, there goes my contribution to your hospital. Of course, the gift carries the compliments of my employer, Captain John. That red-headed boy delivered my messages, I reckon? Well, now, make out that I'm somebody that's come a long way, and that you're tickled to death to see me, and order the fatted calf killed. Otherwise, I won't even dismount."

CHAPTER V.
A FALL OF CRUMBS

An active day followed. The two trail foremen left early to overtake their herds, and the trio at the homestead was fully employed. The cripples were brought up, brands were copied, and the commissary stores assorted and arranged. Before leaving, the men had stretched the sunshade, and the wounded magician sat in state before his own tent door.

The second contingent numbered forty cattle. Like the first, they were a mixed lot, with the exception of a gentle cow. Occasionally a trail foreman would provide his outfit with a milk cow before starting, or gentle one en route, and Seay had willingly given his cow to the hospital on the Beaver.

A fine rain fell during the night. It began falling during the twilight of evening, gathering in force as the hours passed, and only ceased near the middle of the following forenoon. The creek filled to its banks, the field and garden freshened in a day, and the new ranch threw off the blight of summer drouth.

"This will bring the herds," said Forrest, as the sun burst forth at noon. "It's a general rain, and every one in Dodge, now that water is sure, will pull out for the Platte River. It will cool the weather and freshen the grass, and every drover with herds on the trail will push forward for Ogalalla. We'll have to patrol the crossing on the Beaver, as the rain will lay the dust for a week and rob us of our signal."

The crippled man's words proved prophetic. One of the boys was daily detailed to ride to the first divide south, from which a herd, if timing its march to reach the Beaver within a day, could be sighted. On a primal trace, like the Texas and Montana cattle trail, every benefit to the herd was sought, and the freshened range and running water were a welcome breeze to the drover's sail.

The first week after the rain only three herds reached the Beaver. Each foreman paid his respects to Forrest at the homestead, but the herds were heavy beef cattle, purchased at Dodge for delivery on army contracts, and were outfitted anew on a change of owners. The usual flotsam of crippled and stray cattle, of galled and lame saddle stock, and of useless commissary supplies, was missing, and only the well wishes of the wayfaring were left to hearten man and boy at the new ranch.

The second week brought better results. Four of Don Lovell's herds passed within two days, and the nucleus of cattle increased to one hundred and forty odd, seven crippled horses were left, while the commissary stores fairly showered, a second wagon load being necessary to bring up the cache from the trail crossing. In all, during the week, fifteen herds passed, only three of which refused the invitation to call, while one was merely drifting along in search of a range to take up and locate with a herd of cattle. Its owners, new men in the occupation, were scouting wide, and when one of them discovered Hackberry Grove above the homestead, his delight was unbounded, as the range met every requirement for establishing a ranch.

The tyro's exultation was brief. On satisfying himself on the source of the water, the splendid shade and abundance of fuel, he rode down the creek to intercept the trail, and on rounding a bend of the Beaver, was surprised to sight a bunch of cattle. Knowing the value of the range, Forrest had urged the boys to nurse the first contingent of strays up the creek, farther and farther, until they were then ranging within a mile of the grove. The newcomer could hardly control his chagrin, and as he rode along, scarcely a mile was passed but more cattle were encountered, and finally the tent and homestead loomed in sight.

"Well, I'm glad to have such near neighbors," affably said the stranger, as he dismounted before the tent. "Holding down a homestead, I suppose?"

Only Joel and Forrest were at home. "Not exactly," replied the latter; "this is headquarters ranch of Wells Brothers; range from the trail crossing on Beaver to the headwaters of the same. On the trail with cattle, I reckon?"

"Just grazing along until a range can be secured," replied the man. "I've found a splendid one only a few miles up the creek--fine grove of timber and living springs. If the range suits my partner, we'll move in within a few days and take possession."

"Notice any cattle as you came down the creek?" politely inquired Forrest.

"Just a few here and there. They look like strays; must have escaped from some trail herd. If we decide to locate above, I'll have them all rounded up and pushed down the creek."

Joel scented danger as a cub wolf scents blood. He crossed the arbor and took up a position behind Forrest's chair. The latter was a picture of contentment, smiling at the assurance of his caller, and qualifying his remarks with rare irony.

"Well, since you expect to be our neighbor, better unsaddle and stay for dinner," urged Forrest. "Let's get acquainted--at least, come to some friendly understanding."

"No, thank you. My partner is waiting my return to the herd, and will be anxious for my report on the range above. If possible, we don't care to locate any farther north."

"You ought to have secured your range before you bought your cattle. You seem to have the cart before the horse," observed the wounded man.

"Oh," said the novice, with a sweeping gesture, "there's plenty of unclaimed range. There's ample grass and water on this creek to graze five thousand cattle."

"Wells Brothers estimate that the range, tributary to the Beaver, will carry ten thousand head the year round," replied Forrest, languidly indifferent.

"Who are Wells Brothers?" inquired the newcomer.

Forrest turned to the stranger as if informing a child. "You have the name correct," said he. "The brothers took this range some time ago, and those cattle that you met up the creek are theirs. Before you round up any cattle and drive them out, you had better look into the situation thoroughly. You surely know and respect range customs."

"Well," said the stranger explosively,--they mustn't expect to hold the whole country with a handful of cattle."

"They only took the range recently, and are acquiring cattle as fast as possible," politely replied Forrest.

"They can't hold any more country than they can occupy," authoritatively asserted the novice. "All we want is a range for a thousand cows, and I've decided on that hackberry grove as headquarters."

"Your hearing seems defective," remarked Forrest in flute-like tones. "Let me repeat: This is headquarters for Wells Brothers. Their range runs from the trail crossing, six miles below, to the headwaters of Beaver, including all its tributaries. Since you can't stay for dinner, you'll have time to ride down to the crossing of the Texas and Montana trail on this creek. There you'll find the posted notice, so that he who runs may read, that Wells Brothers have already claimed this range. I'll furnish you a pencil and scrap of paper, and you can make a copy of the formal notice and show it to your partner. Then, if you feel strong enough to outrage all range customs, move in and throw down your glove. I've met an accident recently, leaving me a cripple, but I'll agree to get in the saddle and pick up the gauntlet."

The novice led his horse aside as if to mount. "I fail to see the object in claiming more range than one can occupy. It raises a legal question," said he, mounting.

"Custom is the law of the range," replied Forrest. "The increase of a herd must be provided for, and a year or two's experience of beginners like you usually throws cattle on the market. Abundance of range is a good asset. Joel, get the gentleman a pencil and sheet of paper."

"Not at all necessary," remarked the amateur cowman, reining away. "I suppose the range is for sale?" he called out, without halting.

"Yes, but folks who prefer to intrude are usually poor buyers," shouted the crippled Texan.

Joel was alarmed and plied Forrest with a score of questions. The boy had tasted the thrill of ownership of cattle and possession of a range, and now the envy of others had threatened his interests.

"Don't be alarmed," soothingly said the wounded man. "This is like a page from life, only twice as natural. It proves two things: that you took your range in good time, and that it has a value. This very afternoon you must push at least one hundred cattle up to those springs above Hackberry Grove. Let them track and trample around the water and noon in the shade of the motte. That's possession, and possession is nine points, and the other fellow can have the tenth. If any one wants to dispute your rights or encroach on them, I'll mount a horse and go to the trail for help. The Texans are the boys to insist on range customs being respected. It's time I was riding a little, anyhow."

Dell returned from scouting the trail, and reported two herds due to reach the Beaver that evening. "I spent an hour with one of the foremen around the ford," said he to Forrest; "and he says if you want to see him, you had better come down to the crossing. He knows you, and makes out you ain't much hurt. He says if you come down, he'll give you a quarter of beef and a speckled heifer. He's one of Jess Pressnell's bosses."

"That's the word I'm waiting for," laughed Forrest. "Corral the horses and fix up some kind of a mounting block. It'll take a scaffold to get me on a horse, but I can fall off. Make haste, because hereafter we must almost live on horseback."

The words proved true. Forrest and Dell, the latter bareback, returned to the trail, while Joel rode to drift their cattle up the Beaver, in order to be in possession of Hackberry Grove and its living springs. The plains of the West were a lawless country, and if its pioneers would not respect its age-old pastoral customs, then the consequences must be met or borne.

Three weeks had passed since the accident to Forrest, the herds were coming with a vengeance, and the scene of activity changed from the homestead to the trail crossing. Forrest did not return for a week, foraging on the wagons, camping with the herds, and never failing to levy, to the extent of his ability to plead, on cattle, horses, and needful supplies. As many as five and six herds arrived in a single day, none of which were allowed to pass without an appeal: if strangers, in behalf of a hospital; if among friends, the simple facts were sufficient. Dell was kept on the move with bunches of cattle, or freighting the caches to the homestead, while Joel received the different contingents and scouted the threatened range.

Among old acquaintances there was no denying Forrest, and Dell fell heir to the first extra saddle found among the effects of a trail outfit. The galled horses had recovered serviceable form, affording each of the boys a mount, and even the threatened cloud against the range lifted. The herd of a thousand cows crossed the Beaver, and Forrest took particular pains to inform its owners of the whereabouts of unclaimed range the year before. Evidently the embryo cowmen had taken heed and inquired into range customs, and were accordingly profuse with disclaimers of any wrong intent.

The first three weeks of July saw the bulk of the herds north of the Beaver. Water and range had been taken advantage of in the trailing of cattle to the Northwest, fully three hundred thousand head having crossed from Dodge to Ogalalla. The exodus afforded the boys an insight into pastoral life, brought them in close contact with the men of the open, drove false ideas from their immature minds, and assisted in the laying of those early foundations on which their future manhood must rest.

Dell spent every chance hour with the trail men. He and Forrest slept with the wagons, met the herds, and piloted them in to the best water. The fact that only experienced men were employed on the trail made the red-headed boy a welcome guest with every herd, while the wide acquaintance of his crippled sponsor assured the lad every courtesy of camp and road. Dell soon learned that the position of point man usually fell to a veteran of the range, and one whose acquaintance was worthy of cultivation, both in the saddle and around the camp-fire.

"I'm going to be a point man," Dell confided to Forrest, on one of their trips up to the homestead. "He don't seem to have much to do, and nearly always rides with one leg across his horse's neck."

"That's the idea," assented Forrest. "Aim high. Of course, you'll have to begin as a drag man, then a few trips to Montana in the swing, and after that you have a right to expect a place on the point. The trouble is, you are liable to slip back a notch or two at any time. Here I've been a foreman in other years, and this trip I was glad to make a hand. There's so many slips, and we can't be all point men and bosses. Cooks and horse wranglers are also useful men."

The first serious cloud to hover over the new ranch appeared early during the last week in July. Forrest's wounds had nearly healed, and he was wondering if his employer would make a further claim on his services during that summer, which was probable at the hands of a drover with such extensive interests. He and Dell were still patrolling the ford on Beaver, when one evening a conveyance from the railroad to the south drove up to the crossing. It brought a telegram from Don Lovell, requesting the presence of Forrest in Dodge City, and the messenger, a liveryman from Buffalo, further assured him that transportation was awaiting him at that station. There were no grounds on which to refuse the summons, indefinite and devoid of detail as it was, and preparations were immediately made to return with the liveryman. What few cattle had been secured during that trip were drifted up the creek, when all returned to the homestead for the night.

To Dell and Joel the situation looked serious. The crippled man, helpless as he was at first, had proven their rock of refuge, and now that he was leaving them, a tenderness of unnoticed growth was revealed. As an enforced guest, he had come to them at a moment when their poverty had protested at receiving him, his unselfishness in their behalf had proven his friendship and gratitude beyond question, and the lesson was not lost on the parentless waifs.

On the other hand, Forrest lightened all depression of spirits. "Don't worry," said he to the boys. "Just as sure as water runs and grass grows, I'll come over this trail again. So far in life, I've never done any good for myself, and I'm going to play this hand out and see if you lads land on your feet. Now, don't get the idea that I've done any great feat in rustling you boys a few cows. It's one of the laws of life, that often we can do for others what we can't do for ourselves. That sounds like preaching, but it isn't. Actually, I'm ashamed of myself, that I didn't get you double the number of cattle. What we did skirmish together was merely the flotsam of the trail, the crumbs that fall from the supper table, and all obligations to me are overpaid. If I could have had just a few tears on tap, with that hospital talk, and you boys being poor and orphans--shucks! I must be getting doty--that plea was good for a thousand strays and cripples!"

The brothers took courage. So far their chief asset was a fine range. Nearly three hundred and fifty cattle, imperfect as the titles to many of them were, had been secured and were occupying the valley. A round dozen cow ponies, worthless for the present, but which in time would round into form, were added to the new ranch. Every passing commissary had laughed at the chance to discard its plunder and useless staples, and only the departure of the man behind the venture, standing in the shadow as it were, threw a depression over the outlook.

Funds, with which to pay his reckoning, had been left with Forrest. The boys had forgotten the original agreement, and it was only with tact and diplomacy that a snug sum, against his protest and embarrassment, was forced on Joel. "It don't come off me," said the departing man, "and it may come handy with you. There's a long winter ahead, and the fight ain't near won yet. The first year in starting a ranch is always the hardest. But if you boys can only hold these cattle until grass comes again, it's the making of you. You know the boy is father to the man, and if you are true-blue seed corn--well, I'll bet on two ears to the stock."

Forrest's enthusiasm tempered the parting. The start for the railroad was made at daybreak, and in taking leave, each boy held a hand, shaking it heartily from time to time, as if to ratify the general advice. "I'll make Dodge in two days," said the departing guest, "and then I'll know the meaning of this wire. It means something--that's sure. In the mean time, sit square in your saddles, ride your range, and let the idea run riot that you are cowmen. Plan, scheme, and devise for the future. That's all until you hear from me or see my sign in the sky. Adios, señors."

CHAPTER VI.
SUNSHINE AND SHADOW

An entire week passed, during which the boys were alone. A few herds were still coming over the trail, but for lack of an advocate to plead, all hope of securing more cattle must be foregone. Forrest had only taken his saddle, abandoning for the present all fixtures contributed for his comfort on arriving at the homestead, including the horses of his employers. The lads were therefore left an abundance of mounts, all cattle were drifted above the ranch, and plans for the future considered.

Winter must be met and confronted. "We must have forage for our saddle horses," said Joel to his brother, the evening after Forrest's departure. "The rain has helped our corn until it will make fodder, but that isn't enough. Pa cut hay in this valley, and I know where I can mow a ton any morning. Mr. Quince said we'd have to stable a saddle horse apiece this winter, and those mules will have to be fed. The grass has greened up since the rain, and it will be no trick at all to make ten to fifteen tons of hay. Help me grind the scythe, and we'll put in every spare hour haying. While you ride around the cattle every morning, I can mow."

A farm training proved an advantage to the boys. Before coming West, their father had owned a mowing machine, but primitive methods prevailed on the frontier, and he had been compelled to use a scythe in his haying operations. Joel swung the blade like a veteran, scattering his swath to cure in the sun, and with whetstone on steel, beat a frequent tattoo. The raking into windrows and shocking at evening was an easy task for the brothers, no day passing but the cured store was added to, until sufficient was accumulated to build a stack. That was a task which tried their mettle, but once met and overcome, it fortified their courage to meet other ordeals.

"I wish Mr. Quince could see that stack of hay," admiringly said Dell, on the completion of the first effort. "There must be five tons in it. And it's as round as an apple. I can't remember when I've worked so hard and been so hungry. No wonder the Texan despises any work he can't do on horseback. But just the same, they're dear, good fellows. I wish Mr. Quince could live with us always. He's surely a good forager."

The demand for range was accented anew. One evening two strangers rode up the creek and asked for a night's lodging. They were made welcome, and proved to be Texas cowmen, father and son, in search of pasturage for a herd of through cattle. There was an open frankness about the wayfarers that disarmed every suspicion of wrong intent, and the brothers met their inquiries with equal candor.

"And you lads are Wells Brothers?" commented the father, in kindly greeting. "We saw your notice, claiming this range, at the trail crossing, and followed your wagon track up the creek. Unless the market improves, we must secure range for three thousand two-year-old steers. Well, we'll get acquainted, anyhow."

The boys naturally lacked commercial experience in their new occupation. The absence of Forrest was sorely felt, and only the innate kindness of the guests allayed all feeling of insecurity. As the evening wore on, the old sense of dependence brought the lads in closer touch with the strangers, the conversation running over the mutual field of range and cattle matters.

"What is the reason," inquired Joel, "that so many cattle are leaving your State for the upper country?"

"The reasons are numerous and valid," replied the older cowman. "It's the natural outgrowth or expansion of the pastoral interests of our State. Before the opening of the trail, for years and years, Texas clamored for an outlet for its cattle. Our water supply was limited, the State is subject to severe drouth, the cattle were congesting on our ranges, with neither market inquiry or demand. The subjection of the Indian was followed by a sudden development of the West, the Texas and Montana cattle trail opened, and the pastoral resources of our State surprised the world. Last year we sent eight hundred thousand cattle over the trail, and they were not missed at home. That's the reason I'm your guest to-night; range has suddenly become valuable in Texas."

"There is also an economic reason for the present exodus of cattle," added the young man. "Our State is a natural breeding ground, but we can't mature into marketable beef. Nearly twenty years' experience has proven that a northern climate is necessary to fatten and bring our Texas cattle to perfect maturity. Two winters in the North will insure a gain of from three to four hundred pounds' extra weight more per head than if allowed to reach maturity on their native heath. This gain fully doubles the value of every hoof, and is a further motive why we are your guests to-night; we are looking for a northern range on which to mature our steer cattle."

The boys were grasping the fact that in their range they had an asset of value. Less than two months before, they were on the point of abandoning their home as worthless, not capable of sustaining life, the stone which the builders rejected, and now it promised a firm foundation to their future hopes. The threatened encroachment of a few weeks previous, and the causes of demand, as explained by their guests, threw a new light on range values and made the boys doubly cautious. Was there a possible tide in the primitive range, which taken at its flood would lead these waifs to fortune?

The next morning the guests insisted on looking over the upper valley of the Beaver.

"In the first place," said the elder Texan, "let it be understood that we respect your rights to this range. If we can reach some mutual agreement, by purchase or rental, good enough, but not by any form of intrusion. We might pool our interests for a period of years, and the rental would give you lads a good schooling. There are many advantages that might accrue by pooling our cattle. At least, there is no harm in looking over the range."

"They can ride with me as far as Hackberry Grove," said Dell. "None of our cattle range over a mile above the springs, and from there I can nearly point out the limits of our ranch."

"You are welcome to look over the range," assentingly said Joel, "but only on condition that any agreement reached must be made with Mr. Quince Forrest, now at Dodge."

"That will be perfectly agreeable," said the older cowman. "No one must take any advantage of you boys."

The trio rode away, with Dell pointing out around the homestead the different beaver dams in the meanderings of the creek. Joel resumed his mowing, and near noon sighted a cavalcade of horses coming down the dim road which his father used in going to Culbertson. A wagon followed, and from its general outlines the boy recognized it to be a cow outfit, heading for their improvements. Hastening homeward, he found Paul Priest, the gray-haired foreman, who had passed northward nearly two months before, sitting under the sunshade before the tent.

"Howdy, bud," said Priest languidly in greeting. "Now, let me think-- Howdy, Joel!"

No prince could have been more welcome. The men behind the boys had been sadly missed, and the unexpected appearance of Priest filled every want. "Sit down," said the latter. "First, don't bother about getting any dinner; my outfit will make camp on the creek, and we'll have a little spread. Yes, I know; Forrest's in Dodge; old man Don told me he needed him. Where's your brother?"

"Dell's gone up the creek with some cowmen from Texas," admitted Joel. "They're looking for a range. I told them any agreement reached must be made with Mr. Quince. But now that you are here, you will do just as well. They'll be in soon."

"I'm liable to tell them to ride on," said the gray-haired foreman. "I'm jealous, and I want it distinctly understood that I'm a silent partner in this ranch. How many cattle have you?"

"Nearly three hundred and fifty, not counting the calves."

"Forrest only rustled you three hundred and fifty cattle? The lazy wretch--he ought to be hung for ingratitude!"

"Oh, no," protested Joel; "Mr. Quince has been a father to Dell and myself."

"Wait until I come back from Dodge, and I'll show you what a rustler I am," said Priest, arising to give his horse to the wrangler and issue directions in regard to camping.

The arrival of Dell and the cowmen prevented further converse between Priest and his protégé. For the time being a soldier's introduction sufficed between the Texans, but Dell came in for a rough caress. "What do you think of the range?" inquired the trail foreman, turning to the men, and going direct to the subject.

"It meets every requirement for ranching," replied the elder cowman, "and I'm going to make these boys a generous offer."

"This man will act for us," said Joel to the two cowmen, with a jerk of his thumb toward Priest.

"Well, that's good," said the older man, advancing to Priest. "My name is Allen, and this is my son Hugh."

"And my name is Priest, a trail foreman in the employ of Don Lovell," said the gray-haired man, shaking hands with the Texans.

"Mr. Lovell was expected in Dodge the day we left," remarked the younger man in greeting. "We had hopes of selling him our herd."

"What is your county?" inquired the trail boss, searching his pockets for a telegram.

"Comanche."

"And when did you leave Dodge?"

"Just ten days ago."

"Then you need no range--your cattle are sold," said Priest, handing the older man a telegram.

The two scanned the message carefully, and the trail foreman continued: "This year my herd was driven to fill a sub-contract, and we delivered it last week at old Camp Clark, on the North Platte. From there the main contractor will trail the beef herd up to the Yellowstone. Old man Don was present at the delivery, and when I got back to Ogalalla with the oufit, that message was awaiting me. I'm now on my way to Dodge to receive the cattle. They go to the old man's beef ranch on the Little Missouri. It says three thousand Comanche County two-year-olds, don't it?"

"It's our cattle," said the son to his father. "We have the only straight herd of Comanche County two-year-olds at Dodge City. That commission man said he would sell them before we got back."

The elder Texan turned to the boys with a smile. "I reckon we'll have to declare all negotiations off regarding this range. I had several good offers to make you, and I'm really sorry at this turn of events. I had figured out a leasing plan, whereby the rentals of this range would give you boys a fine schooling, and revert to you on the eldest attaining his majority. We could have pooled our cattle, and your interests would have been carried free."

"You needn't worry about these boys," remarked Priest, with an air of interest; "they have silent partners. As to schooling, I've known some mighty good men who never punched the eyes out of the owl in their old McGuffy spelling-book."

A distant cry of dinner was wafted up the creek. "That's a welcome call," said Priest, arising. "Come on, everybody. My cook has orders to tear his shirt in getting up a big dinner."

A short walk led to the camp. "This outfit looks good to me," said the elder cowman to Priest, "and you can count on my company to the railroad."

"You're just the man I'm looking for," replied the trail boss. "We're making forty miles a day, and you can have charge until we reach Dodge."

"But I only volunteered as far as the railroad," protested the genial Texan.

"Yes; but then I know you cowmen," contended Priest. "You have lived around a wagon so long and love cow horses so dearly, that you simply can't quit my outfit to ride on a train. Two o'clock is the hour for starting, and I'll overtake you before evening."

The outfit had been reduced to six men, the remainder having been excused and sent home from Ogalalla. The remuda was in fine condition, four changes of mounts a day was the rule, and on the hour named, the cavalcade moved out, leaving its foreman behind. "Angle across the plain and enter the trail on the divide, between here and the Prairie Dog," suggested Priest to his men. "We will want to touch here coming back, and the wagon track will point the way. Mr. Allen will act as segundo."

Left to themselves, the trio resolved itself into a ways and means committee. "I soldiered four years," said Priest to the boys, once the sunshade was reached, "and there's nothing that puts spirit and courage into the firing line like knowing that the reserves are strong. It's going to be no easy task to hold these cattle this winter, and now is the time to bring up the ammunition and provision the camp. The army can't march unless the mules are in condition, and you must be well mounted to handle cattle. Ample provision for your saddle stock is the first requirement."

"We're putting up a ton of hay a day," said Joel, "and we'll have two hundred shocks of fodder."

"That's all right for rough forage, but you must have corn for your saddle stock," urged the man. "Without grain for the mounts, cavalry is useless. I think the railroad supplies, to settlers along its line, coal, lumber, wire, and other staples at cost. I'll make inquiry to-morrow and let you know when we return. One hundred bushels of corn would make the forage reserves ample for the winter."

"We've got money enough to buy it," admitted Joel. "I didn't want to take it, but Mr. Quince said it would come in handy."

"That covers the question of forage, then," said Priest. "Now comes the question of corrals and branding."

"Going to brand the calves?" impulsively inquired Dell, jumping at conclusions.

"The calves need not be branded before next spring," replied the practical man, "but the herd must be branded this fall. If a blizzard struck the cattle on the open, they would drift twenty miles during a night. These through Texas cattle have been known to drift five hundred miles during the first winter. You must guard against a winter drift, and the only way is to hold your cattle under herd. If you boys let these cattle out of your hand, away from your control, they'll drift south to the Indian reservations and be lost. You must hold them in spite of storms, and you will need a big, roomy inclosure in which to corral the herd at night."

"There's the corn field," suggested Dell.

"It has no shelter," objected Priest. "Your corral must protect against the north and west winds."

"The big bend's the place," said Joel. "The creek makes a perfect horseshoe, with bluff banks almost twenty feet high on the north and northwest. One hundred yards of fencing would inclose five acres. Our cows used to shelter there. It's only a mile above the house."

"What's the soil, and how about water?" inquired the gray-haired foreman, arising.

"It's a sand-bar, with a ripple and two long pools in the circle of the creek," promptly replied Joel.

"Bring in the horses," said Priest, looking at his watch; "I'll have time to look it over before leaving."

While awaiting the horses, the practical cowman outlined to Joel certain alterations to the corral at the stable, which admitted of the addition of a branding chute. "You must cut and haul the necessary posts and timber before my return, and when we pass north, my outfit will build you a chute and brand your cattle the same day. Have the materials on the ground, and I'll bring any needful hardware from the railroad."

A short canter brought the committee to the big bend. The sand-bar was overgrown with weeds high as a man's shoulder on horseback, but the leader, followed by the boys, forced his mount through the tangle until the bend was circled. "It's an ideal winter shelter," said Priest, dismounting to step the entrance, as a preliminary measurement. "A hundred and ten yards," he announced, a few minutes later, "coon-skin measurement. You'll need twenty heavy posts and one hundred stays. I'll bring you a roll of wire. That water's everything; a thirsty cow chills easily. Given a dry bed and contented stomach, in this corral your herd can laugh at any storm. It's almost ready made, and there's nothing niggardly about its proportions."

"When will we put the cattle under herd?" inquired Dell as the trio rode homeward.

"Oh, about the second snowstorm," replied Priest. "After squaw winter's over, there's usually a month to six weeks of Indian summer. It might be as late as the first of December, but it's a good idea to loose-herd awhile; ride around them evening and morning, corral them and leave the gates open, teach them to seek a dry, cosy bed, at least a month before putting the cattle under close-herd. Teach them to drink in the corral, and then they'll want to come home. You boys will just about have to live with your little herd this winter."

"We wintered here once," modestly said Joel, "and I'm sure we can do it again. The storms are the only thing to dread, and we can weather them."

"Of course you can," assured the trail boss. "It's a ground-hog case; it's hold these cattle or the Indians will eat them for you. Lost during one storm, and your herd is lost for good."

"And about horses: will one apiece be enough?" queried Joel. "Mr. Quince thought two stabled ones would do the winter herding."

"One corn-fed pony will do the work of four grass horses," replied the cowman. "Herding is no work for horses, provided you spare them. If you must, miss your own dinner, but see that your horse gets his. Dismount and strip the bridle off at every chance, and if you guard against getting caught out in storms, one horse apiece is all you need."

On reaching the homestead, Priest shifted his saddle to a horse in waiting, and announced his regrets at being compelled to limit his visit. "It may be two weeks before I return," said he, leading his horse from the corral to the tent, "but we'll point in here and lend a hand in shaping you up for winter. Forrest is liable to have a herd of his own, and in that case, there will be two outfits of men. More than likely, we'll come through together."

Hurried as he professed to be, the trail foreman pottered around as if time was worthless, but finally mounted. "Now the commissary is provisioned," said he, in summing up the situation, "to stand a winter's siege, the forage is ample, the corral and branding chute is half done--well, I reckon we're the boys to hold a few cattle. Honest Injun, I hope it will storm enough this winter to try you out; just to see what kind of thoroughbreds you really are. And if any one else offers to buy an interest in this range," he called back, as a happy afterthought, "just tell them that you have all the partners you need."

CHAPTER VII.
ALL IN THE DAY'S WORK

The brief visit of Priest proved a tonic to the boys. If a firing line of veteran soldiers can be heartened, surely the spirit and courage of orphan waifs needed fortifying against the coming winter. The elements have laughed at the hopes and ambitions of a conqueror, and an invincible army has trailed its banners in the snow, unable to cope with the rigors of the frost king. The lads bent anew to their tasks with a cheerfulness which made work mere play, sweetening their frugal fare, and bringing restful sleep. The tie which began in a mercenary agreement had seemingly broken its bonds, and in lieu, through the leaven of human love, a new covenant had been adopted.

"If it's a dry, open winter," said Dell at breakfast next morning, "holding these cattle will be nothing. The water holds them now without herding."

"Yes," replied Joel, "but we must plan to meet the worst possible winter. A blizzard gives little warning, and the only way to overcome one is to be fully prepared. That's what Mr. Paul means by bringing up the ammunition. We must provide so as to be able to withstand a winter siege."

"Well, what's lacking?" insisted Dell.

"Fuel. Take an axe with you this morning, and after riding around the cattle, cut and collect the dead and fallen timber in Hackberry Grove. Keep an eye open for posts and stays--I'll cut them while you're hauling wood. Remember we must have the materials on the ground when Mr. Paul returns, to build a corral and branding chute."

Axe and scythe were swung that morning with renewed energy. Within a week the required amount of hay was in stack, while the further supply of forage, promised in the stunted corn, was daily noted in its advancing growth.

Without delay the scene of activity shifted. The grove was levied on, a change of axe-men took place, while the team even felt a new impetus by making, instead of one, two round trips daily. The fuel supply grew, not to meet a winter's, but a year's requirements. Where strength was essential, only the best of timber was chosen, and well within the time limit the materials for corral and branding chute were at hand on the ground. One task met and mastered, all subsequent ones seemed easier.

"We're ahead of time," said Joel with a quiet air of triumph, as the last load of stays reached the corral site. "If we only knew the plans, we might dig the post-holes. The corn's still growing, and it won't do to cut until it begins to ripen--until the sugar rises in the stock. We can't turn another wheel until Mr. Paul returns."

Idleness was galling to Joel Wells. "We'll ride the range to-day," he announced the following morning. "From here to the ford doesn't matter, but all the upper tributaries ought to be known. We must learn the location of every natural shelter. If a storm ever cuts us off from the corrals, we must point the herd for some other port."

"The main Beaver forks only a few miles above Hackberry Grove," suggested Dell.

"Then we'll ride out the south fork to-day and come back through the sand hills. There must be some sheltered nooks in that range of dunes."

That the morning hour has gold in its mouth, an unknown maxim at the new ranch, mattered nothing. The young cowmen were up and away with the rising sun, riding among and counting the different bunches of cattle encountered, noting the cripples, and letting no details of the conditions of the herd, in their leisurely course up the creek, escape their vigilance.

The cattle tallied out to an animal, and were left undisturbed on their chosen range. Two hours' ride brought the boys to the forks of the Beaver, and by the middle of the forenoon the south branch of the creek was traced to its source among the sand dunes. If not inviting, the section proved interesting, with its scraggy plum brush, its unnumbered hills, and its many depressions, scalloped out of the sandy soil by the action of winds. Coveys of wild quail were encountered, prairie chicken took wing on every hand, and near the noon hour a monster gray wolf arose from a sunny siesta on the summit of a near-by dune, and sniffed the air in search of the cause of disturbance. Unseen, the boys reined in their horses, a windward breeze favored the view for a moment, when ten nearly full-grown cubs also arose and joined their mother in scenting the horsemen. It was a rare glimpse of wary beasts, and like a flash of light, once the human scent was detected, mother and whelps skulked and were lost to sight in an instant.

"They're an enemy of cattle," whispered Joel when the cubs appeared. "The young ones are not old enough yet to hunt alone, and are still following their mother. Their lair is in these hills, and if this proves a cold winter, hunger will make them attack our cattle before spring. We may have more than storms to fight. There they go."

"How are we to fight them?" timidly asked Dell. "We have neither dog nor gun."

"Mr. Paul will know," replied Joel with confidence. "They'll not bother us while they can get food elsewhere."

The shelter of a wolf-pack's lair was not an encouraging winter refuge to drifting cattle. The boys even shook out their horses for a short gallop in leaving the sand dunes, and breathed easier once the open of the plain was reached. Following a low watershed, the brothers made a wide detour from the Beaver, but on coming opposite the homestead, near the middle of the afternoon, they turned and rode directly for the ranch, where a welcome surprise greeted them.

Four men were at work on the branding chute. A single glance revealed both Priest and Forrest among the quartette. On riding up to the stable corral, in the rough reception which followed, the lads were fairly dragged from their saddles amid hearty greetings. "Well, here we are again, and as busy as cranberry merchants," said Priest, once order was restored.

"Where's your herd?" inquired Joel.

"He hasn't any," interrupted Forrest; "he's working for me. About this time to-morrow evening, I'll split this ranch wide open with two herds, each of thirty-five hundred two-year-old steers. I'm coming with some style this time. You simply can't keep a good man down."

"There were two herds instead of one to go to the old man's beef ranch," explained Priest. "We brought along a couple extra men and came through a day ahead. We can't halt our cattle, but we can have the chute and corrals nearly ready when the herds arrive. All we'll lack is the hardware, and the wagons will reach here early during the afternoon."

The homestead presented a busy scene for the remainder of the day. Every old tool on the ranch was brought into service, and by twilight the outlines of the branding chute had taken form. The stable corral was built out of heavy poles and posts, with a capacity of holding near one hundred cattle, and by a very slight alteration it could be enlarged, with branding conveniences added.

At this point it was deemed advisable to enlighten the boys regarding the title of stray cattle. Forrest and Priest had talked the matter over between themselves, and had decided that the simple truth concerning the facts was the only course to adopt. The older of the two men, by the consent of years, was delegated to instruct the lads, and when the question of brands to be adopted by the new ranch was under consideration, the chance presented itself.

"In starting this ranch," said the gray-haired foreman to the boys, as they all sat before the tent in the twilight, "we'll have to use two brands. Cattle are conveyed from one owner to another by bill-of-sale. In a big pastoral exodus like the present, it is simply impossible to keep strays out of moving herds. They come in at night, steal in while a herd is passing through thickets, while it is watering, and they may not be noticed for a month. Under all range customs, strays are recognized as flotsam. Title is impossible, and the best claim is due to the range that gives them sustenance. It has always been customary to brand the increase of strays to the range on which they are found, and that will entitle you to all calves born of stray mothers."

The brothers were intent listeners, and the man continued: "For fear of winter drifting, and that they may be identified, we will run all these strays into Two Bars on the left hip, which will be known as the 'Hospital' brand. For the present, that will give us an asylum for that branch of flotsam gathered, and as trustees and owners of the range, all increase will fall to Wells Brothers. However, in accepting this deputyship, you do so with the understanding that the brand is merely a tally-mark, and that in no way does it deprive the owner of coming forward to prove and take possession of his property. This method affords a refuge to all strays in your possession, and absolves you from any evil intent. All other cattle coming under your control, with the knowledge and consent of the owner or his agent, are yours in fee simple, and we will run them into any brand you wish to adopt."

"But suppose no one ever calls for these stray cows?" said Joel, meditating.

"Then let them live out their days in peace," advised Forrest. "The weeds grow rankly wherever a cow dies, and that was the way their ancestors went. One generation exempts you."

The discovery of wolves in that immediate vicinity was not mentioned until the following morning. The forces were divided between the tasks, and as Priest and Joel rode up the valley to the site of the new corral, the disclosure was made known.

"Wolves? Why, certainly," said Priest, answering his own query. "Wolves act as a barometer in forecasting the coming of storms. Their activity or presence will warn you of the approach of blizzards, and you want to take the hint and keep your weather eye open. When other food becomes scarce, they run in packs and will kill cattle. You are perfectly safe, as yours will be either under herd or in a corral. Wolves always single out an animal to attack; they wouldn't dare enter an inclosure. Taken advantage of in their hunger, they can be easily poisoned. A wolf dearly loves kidney suet or fresh tallow, and by mixing strychnine with either, they can be lured to their own destruction."

The post-holes were dug extra deep for the corral. The work was completed before noon, the gate being the only feature of interest. It was made double, fifty feet wide, and fastened in the centre to a strong post. The gate proper was made of wire, webbed together with stays, admitting of a pliability which served a double purpose. By sinking an extra post opposite each of the main ones, the flexibility of the gate also admitted of making a perfect wing, aiding in the entrance or exit of a herd. In fastening the gate in the centre short ropes were used, and the wire web drawn taut to the tension of a pliable fence. "You boys will find this short wing, when penning a herd, equal to an extra man," assured the old foreman.

The first round-up on the new ranch took place that afternoon. Forrest took the extra men and boys, and riding to the extreme upper limits of the range, threw out the drag-net of horsemen and turned homeward. The cattle ranged within a mile or two on either side of the creek, and by slowly closing in and drifting down the Beaver, the nucleus of the ranch was brought into a compact herd. There was no hurry, as ample time must be allowed for the arrival of the wagons and stretching of the wire, in finishing and making ready the upper corral for its first reception of cattle. There was a better reason for delay, which was held in reserve, as a surprise for the boys.

As expected, the wagons and remudas arrived at the new ranch hours in advance of the herds. The horse wranglers were detailed by Priest, and fitting an axle to the spool of wire, by the aid of ropes attached to the pommels of two saddles, it was rolled up to the scene of its use at an easy canter. The stretching of the wire was less than an hour's work, the slack being taken up by the wranglers, ever upholding Texas methods, from the pommels of saddles, while Priest clinched the strands with staples at the proper tension. The gates were merely a pliable extension of the fence, the flexible character requiring no hinges. "Now, when the stays are interwoven through the wire, and fastened in place with staples, there's a corral that will hold a thousand cattle," said one of the wranglers admiringly.

It was after sunset when the herd was penned. Forrest, after counting the round-up to his satisfaction, detailed Dell and Joel to graze the herd in a bend of the Beaver, out of sight and fully a mile above, and taking the extra men returned to the homestead. The trail herds had purposely arrived late, expecting to camp on the Beaver that night, and were met by their respective foremen while watering for the day. In receiving, at Dodge, two large herds of one-aged cattle, both foremen, but more particularly Forrest, in the extra time at his command, had levied on the flotsam of the herds from which his employer was buying, until he had accumulated over one hundred cattle. Priest had secured, among a few friends and the few herds with which he came in contact, scarcely half that number, and still the two contingents made a very material increase to the new ranch.

The addition of these extra cattle was the surprise in reserve. Joel and Dell had never dreamed of a further increase to the ranch stock, and Forrest had timed the corralling of the original and late contingents as the climax of the day's work. Detailing both of the boys on the point, as the upper herd was nearing the corral, it was suddenly confronted by another contingent, rounding a bend of the creek from the opposite quarter. Priest had purposely detailed strange men, coached to the point of blindness, in charge of the new addition, and when the two bunches threatened to mix, every horseman present except the boys seemed blind to the situation.

Dell and Joel struggled in vain--the cattle mixed. "Well, well," said Forrest, galloping up, "here's a nice come-off! Trust my own boys to point a little herd into a corral, and they let two bunches of cattle mix! Wouldn't that make a saint swear!"

"Those other fellows had no man in the lead or on the point," protested Dell dejectedly. "They were looking away off yonder, and their cattle walked into ours. Where were you?"

"One of my men was telling me about an old sweetheart of his down on the Trinity River, and it made me absent-minded. I forgot what we were doing. Well, it's too late in the day to separate them now. We'll pen them until morning."

The appearance of Priest and the readiness with which the strange men assisted in corralling the herd shortly revealed the situation to the crafty Joel. On the homeward canter, the gray-haired foreman managed to drop a word which lightened Dell's depression and cleared up the supposed error.

That was a great night on the Beaver. The two wagons camped together, the herds bedded on either side of the creek, and the outfits mingled around the same camp-fire. Rare stories were told, old songs were sung, the lusty chorus of which easily reached the night-herders, and was answered back like a distant refrain.

The next morning the herds moved out on their way without a wasted step. Two men were detailed from each outfit, and with the foremen and the boys, a branding crew stood ready for the task before them. The chute had been ironed and bolted the evening previous, and long before the early rays of the sun flooded the valley of the Beaver, the first contingent of cattle arrived from the upper corral.

The boys adopted Bar Y as their brand. The chute chambered ten grown cattle, and when clutched in a vise-like embrace, with bars fore and aft, the actual branding, at the hands of two trail foremen, was quickly over. The main herd was cut into half a dozen bunches, and before the noon hour arrived, the last hoof had passed under the running irons and bore the new owner's brand or tally-mark.

Only a short rest was allowed, as the herds were trailing the limit of travel, and must be overtaken by evening. When crossing the railroad a few days before, it was learned that Grinnell was the railroad depot for settlers' supplies, and the boys were advised to file their order for corn, and to advance a liberal payment to insure attention. All details of the ranch seemed well in hand, the cattle were in good condition to withstand a winter, and if spirit and confidence could be imparted, from age to youth, the sponsors of the venture would have felt little concern for the future. If a dry, open winter followed, success was assured; if the reverse, was it right to try out the very souls of these waifs in a wintry crucible?

The foremen and their men left early in the afternoon. On reaching a divide, which gave the party of horsemen a last glimpse of the Beaver, the cavalcade halted for a parting look.

"Isn't it a pretty range?" said Forrest, gazing far beyond the hazy valley. "I wish we knew if those boys can stick out the winter."

"Stick? We'll make them stick!" said Priest, in a tone as decisive as if his own flesh and blood had been insulted.

CHAPTER VIII.
THE LINES OF INTRENCHMENT

The boys watched the cavalcade until it faded away in the swells of the plain. At each recurring departure of their friends, in spite of all bravado to the contrary, a pall of loneliness crept into the hearts of the waifs. Theirs had been a cheerless boyhood; shifted about from pillar to post, with poverty their one sure companion, they had tasted of the wormwood in advance of their years. Toys such as other lads played with for an hour and cast aside were unknown in their lives, and only the poor substitute for hoop, horse, or gun had been theirs. In the struggle for existence, human affection was almost denied them. A happy home they had never known, and the one memory of their childhood worthy of remembrance was the love of a mother, which arose like a lily in the mire of their lives, shedding its fragrance more fully as its loss was realized.

Joel was the more sensitive of the brothers. Forrest had fully discussed the coming winter with the older lad, and as an incentive to watchfulness had openly expressed doubt of the ability of the boys to battle with the elements. The conversation was depressing, and on the departure of the men, the boys resumed the discussion of the matter at issue.

"Mr. Quince thinks we can't hold these cattle," said Joel, watching the receding horsemen. "He's afraid a storm will catch us several miles out and cut us off from reaching the corral. Well, it will be my fault if it does."

Dell made a boastful remark, but the older boy only intensified his gaze at the fading cavalcade. A vision of his youthful sufferings flashed through his mind, and a mist, closely akin to tears, dimmed his eyes. He had learned the lesson that poverty teaches, unaware that the storm which rocks also roots the oak, but unable to make the comparison or draw the inference between surrounding nature and himself. For an instant the horsemen dipped from view, changing the scene, and a picture rose up, a vision of the future, of independence, of a day when he would take his place as a man among men. The past was beyond his control, its bridges burned, but the future was worth battling for; and as if encouraged by invisible helpers, the boy turned his face to the valley of the Beaver.

"We'll hold these cattle or starve," said he, unconsciously answering his gray-haired sponsor, fading from sight over the last divide. "Hold them. I can hold them alone."

"There's no danger of starving," commented Dell, following his brother into the tent. "We have provisions for a year."

"Then we'll hold the herd or freeze," answered Joel, almost hissing the words--words which became a slogan afterward.

The cattle drifted back to their chosen range. The late addition mixed and mingled with the others, now attached to the valley, with its abundance of grass and water. Nothing was said about the first four horses, from which the boys understood that they were, at least for the present, left in their charge. All told, sixteen horses, fully half of which were fit for saddle, were at the service of the ranch, ample in number in proportion to the cattle secured.

It was only the middle of August. An accident, and a little over two months' time, had changed the character of the Beaver valley. With no work pressing, the brothers rode the range, circling farther to the west and south, until any country liable to catch a winter drift became familiar to sight. Northward ho! the slogan of every drover had ceased, and the active trail of a month before had been deserted. The new ranch had no neighbors, the nearest habitation was on the railroad to the south, and the utter loneliness of the plain was only overcome by active work. To those who love them, cattle and horses are good company, and in their daily rides the lads became so familiar with the herd that in the absence of brands they could have readily identified every animal by flesh marks alone. Under almost constant contact with the boys, the cattle became extremely gentle, while the calves even grew so indifferent that they reluctantly arose from their beds to avoid a passing horseman.

The cutting, curing, and garnering home the field of corn was a welcome task. It augmented the forage supply, assuring sustenance to the saddle horses, an important feature in withstanding the coming winter siege. An ideal fall favored the ranch, the dry weather curing the buffalo grass on the divides, until it was the equal of hay, thus assuring the cattle of ample grazing until spring. The usual squaw winter passed in a swirl of snow, a single angry day, to be followed by a month of splendid Indian summer. Its coming warned the lads; the order for corn was placed; once a week the cattle were brought in and corralled, and the ranch was made snug against the wintry months.

The middle of November was as early as the railroad would agree to deliver the corn. It would take three days to go and come, and an equal number of round trips would be required to freight the grain from the railroad to the ranch. The corn had been shelled and sacked at elevator points, eastward in the State, and in encouraging emigration the railroad was glad to supply the grain at cost and freightage.

The hauling fell to Joel. He had placed the order, making a deposit, and identification was necessary with the agent. On the very first trip to Grinnell, a mere station on the plain, a surprise awaited the earnest boy. As if he were a citizen of the hamlet, and in his usual quiet way, Paul Priest greeted Joel on his arrival. The old foreman had secretly left a horse with the railroad agent at Buffalo, where the trail crossed, had kept in touch with the delivery of corn at stations westward, and had timed his affairs so as to meet and pay a final visit to his protégées.

"A battle is sometimes lost by a very slight oversight or accident," said the man to the boy. "The ammunition may get damaged, slippery ground might prevent the placing of a battery at an opportune moment, or the casting of a horse's shoe might delay a courier with an important order. I feel an interest in your little ranch, and when I know that everything is done that can be done to fortify against the coming winter, I'll go home feeling better. There is such a thing as killing the spirit of a soldier, and if I were to let you boys try and fail, it would affect your courage to face the future. That's the reason I've dropped off to take a last look at your lines of intrenchment. We've got to hold those cattle."

"Mr. Quince thinks we won't, but let the winter come as it may, we're going to hold the herd," simply said the boy.

There was a resolution, an earnestness, in the words of the lad that pleased the man. "Your Mr. Quince has seen some cold winters on the range," said the latter, "and that's the reason he fears the worst. But come as it will, if we do all in our power, put up the best fight in us, and fail, then we are blameless. But with my experience, if I let you fail, when you might have won, then I have done you an injury."

That was the platform on which men and boys stood, the outline on which their mutual venture must stand or fall, and admitted of no shirking on the part of any one. The most minute detail, down to a change of clean saddle blankets, for winter work, must be fully understood. The death of a horse in which reliance rested, at an unfortunate moment, might mean the loss of the herd, and a clean, warm blanket on a cold day was the merciful forethought of a man for his beast. No damp, frosty, or frozen blanket must be used on the Wells ranch.

On the return trip, an early start was made. A night camp was necessary, at the halfway point, the dread of which was robbed of its terrors by the presence of a veteran of the open. Before leaving the depot, Priest unearthed a number of bundles, "little things that might come in handy," among which was a sack of salt and two empty oak barrels. The latter provoked an inquiry from Joel, and an explanation was forced at the moment.

"Did you notice a big steer that came in with the last cattle, and which was overlooked in branding?" inquired Priest, meeting the boy's query with a question.

"A mottled beef, branded 7L?"

"That's the steer. Why do you reckon we overlooked branding him?"

"Dell and I thought it was an oversight."

"When you see what I'm going to do with that salt and these barrels, then you'll see that it was no neglect. That steer has undergone several Northern winters, has reached his prime, and the governor's cellar won't have any better corn beef this winter than the Wells ranch. Seven or eight hundred pounds of pickled beef is an important item in the winter intrenchments. In fact, it's an asset to any cow camp. There are so many little things that may come in handy."

The second morning out from the station, Priest bore off on a course that would land him well above the grove on the Beaver. He had never been over the range, and not wishing to waste a day with a loaded wagon, he angled away for the sand hills which formed the divide, sloping away to the branches of the main creek. Noon found him on the south fork; cattle were encountered near the juncture, and as he approached the grove, a horseman rode out as if to dispute the passage of an intruder. The old foreman noticed the boyish figure and delayed the meeting, reining in to critically examine cattle which he had branded some three months before. With diligent intent, the greeting was kept pending, the wayfarer riding away on a tangent and veering back on his general course, until Dell's suspicion was aroused. The return of Priest was so unexpected that the boy's eyes filled with tears, and the two rode along until the grove was reached, when they dismounted.

"If I had known that you were coming," said Dell, "I could have made coffee here. It was so lonesome at the ranch that I was spending the day among the cattle."

"A cowman expects to miss his dinner occasionally," admitted Priest; "that's why they all look so long and hungry. Where does that 7L steer range?"

"The big mottled fellow?--Why, down near the corral," replied the boy, repeating and answering the question.

"I want to look him over," simply said the old foreman.

The two remounted and continued down the valley. The noon hour had brought the herd in for its daily water, and no animal was overlooked on the homeward ride. The summer gloss had passed and the hairy, shaggy, winter coats of the cattle almost hid the brands, while three to six months' rest on a perfect range was reflected in the splendid condition of the general herd.

"That's one feature of the winter intrenchments that needn't worry us," said Priest; "the cattle have the tallow to withstand any ordinary winter."

"And the horses are all rolling fat," added Dell. "They range below the ranch; and there isn't a cripple or sore back among them. There's the mottled steer."

They were nearing the last contingent of cattle. Priest gave the finished animal a single glance, and smiled. "Outsiders say," said he, "that it's a maxim among us Texans never to eat your own beef. The adage is worth transplanting. We'll beef him. The lines of intrenchment are encouraging."

The latter remarks were not fully understood by Dell, but on the arrival of the wagon that evening, and a short confidence between the brothers, the horizon cleared. Aside from the salt and barrels, there were sheepskin-lined coats and mittens, boots of heavy felting, flannels over and under, as if the boys were being outfitted for a polar expedition. "It may all come in handy," said a fatherly voice, "and a soldier out on sentinel duty ought to be made comfortable. In holding cattle this winter, it's part of the intrenchments."

A cyclone cellar served as a storeroom for the sacked corn. Joel was away by early sun-up, on the second trip to the station, while those left behind busied themselves in strengthening the commissary. The barrels were made sweet and clean with scalding water, knives were ground, and a crude platform erected for cooling out meat. Dell, on the tip-toe of expectancy, danced attendance, wondering how this quiet man would accomplish his ends, and unable to wholly restrain his curiosity.

"Watch me closely," was the usual reply. "You will probably marry young, and every head of a family, on a ranch, ought to know how to cure corn beef. Give me a week of frosty nights, and the lesson is yours. Watch me closely."

The climax of the day was felling the beef. Near the middle of the afternoon, the two rode out, cut off a small contingent of cattle, including the animal wanted, and quietly drifted them down to the desired location. Dell's curiosity had given way to alertness, and when the old foreman shook out a rope, the boy instinctively knew that a moment of action was at hand. Without in the least alarming the other cattle, the cast was made, the loop opened in mid-air, settled around the horns, cut fast by a jerk of the rope, and the contest between man and animal began. It was over in a moment. The shade of a willow was the chosen spot, and as the cattle were freed, the steer turned, the horseman taking one side of the tree and the beef the other, wrapping several turns of the rope in circling on contrary courses. The instant the big fellow quieted, on its coming to a level, a pistol flashed, and the beef fell in his tracks. That was the programme--to make the kill in the shade of the willow. And it was so easily done.

"That's about all we can do on horseback," said the gray-haired Texan, dismounting. "You may bring the knives."

Every step in the lesson was of interest to Dell. Before dark the beef was cut into suitable pieces and spread on the platform to drain and cool. During the frosty night following, all trace of animal heat passed away, and before sunrise the meat was salted into barrels. Thereafter, or until it was drained of every animal impurity, the beef was spread on the platform nightly, the brine boiled and skimmed, until a perfect pickle was secured. It was a matter of a week's concern, adding to the commissary two barrels of prime corned beef, an item of no small value in the line of sustenance.

The roping of the beef had not been overlooked. "I can't see what made the loop open for you yesterday," said Dell the next morning; "it won't open for me."

Priest took the rope from the boy. "What the tail means to a kite, or the feather to an arrow," said he, running out an oval noose, "the same principle applies to open the loop of a rope. The oval must have a heavy side, which you get by letting the Hondo run almost halfway round the loop, or double on one side. Then when you make your cast, the light side will follow the heavy, and your loop will open. In other words, what the feather is to the arrow, the light side is to the heavy, and if you throw with force, the loop must open."

It seemed so easy. Like a healthy boy, Dell had an ambition to be a fearless rider and crack roper. During the week which followed, in the saddle or at leisure, the boy never tired of practicing with a rope, while the patient man called attention to several wrist movements which lent assistance in forming a perfect loop. The slightest success was repeated to perfection; unceasing devotion to a task masters it, and before the visit ended, the perfect oval poised in the air and the rope seemingly obeyed the hand of Dell Wells.

"It's all right to master these little details of the cattle business," said Priest to Dell, "but don't play them as lead cards. Keep them up your sleeve, as a private accomplishment, for your own personal use. These fancy riders and ropers are usually Sunday men. When I make up an outfit for the trail, I never insist on any special attainments. Just so he's good natured, and no danger of a rainy night dampening the twinkle in his eye, that's the boy for me. Then if he can think a little, act quick, clear, and to the point, I wouldn't care if he couldn't rope a cow in a month."

In considering the lines of resistance, the possibility of annoyance from wolves was not overlooked. There was an abundance of suet in the beef, several vials of strychnine had been provided, and a full gallon of poisoned tallow was prepared in event of its needs. While Joel was away after the last load of corn, several dozen wooden holders were prepared, two-inch auger holes being sunk to the depth of five or six inches, the length of a wolf's tongue, and the troughs charred and smoked of every trace of human scent.

That the boys might fully understand the many details, the final instructions were delayed until Joel's return. "Always bear in mind that a wolf is a wary beast," admonished Priest, "and match your cunning against his. Make no mistake, take no chances, for you're dealing with a crafty enemy. About the troughs on the ground, surrounding the bait, every trace of human scent must be avoided. For that reason, you must handle the holder with a spear or hay fork, and if you have occasion to dismount, to refill a trough, carry a board to alight on, remembering to lower and take it up by rope, untouched even by a gloved hand. The scent of a horse arouses no suspicion; in fact, it is an advantage, as it allays distrust."

In loading a bait, an object lesson was given, using unpoisoned suet. "After throwing off all suspicion," continued Priest, illustrating the process, "the next thing is to avoid an overdose. An overdose acts as an emetic, and makes a wise wolf. For that reason, you must pack the tallow in the auger hole, filling from a half to two thirds full. Force Mr. Wolf to lick it out, administer the poison slowly, and you are sure of his scalp. You will notice I have bored the hole in solid wood, to prevent gnawing, and you must pack the suet firmly, to prevent spilling, as a crafty wolf will roll a trough over and over to dislodge the bait. Keep your holders out in the open, exposed to the elements, scald the loading tools before using, and you have the upper hand of any wolves that may molest your cattle."

The trail foreman spent a pleasant two weeks at the Wells ranch. After the corn was in store, the trio rode the range and reviewed every possible line of defense. Since the winter could not be foreseen, the only safe course was to anticipate the worst, and barring the burning of the range from unseen sources, the new ranch stood prepared to withstand a winter siege. Everything to forefend against a day of stress or trial had been done, even to instilling courage into youthful hearts.

"There's only one thing further that comes to mind," said the practical man, as they rode homeward, "and that is to face an unexpected storm. If a change of weather threatens, point your herd to meet it, and then if you are caught out, you will have the storm in your back to drift the cattle home. Shepherds practice that rule, and the same applies to cattle under herd."

All horses were to be left at the new ranch for the winter. Dell volunteered to accompany their guest to the railroad and bring back the extra mount, thus leaving five of Lovell's horses in possession of the boys. On the day of departure, at breakfast, after a final summary of the lines of resistance, the trio dallied about the table, the trail foreman seemingly reluctant to leave.

"It's a common remark among us drovers," said Priest, toying with his coffee cup, "that a cowman is supposed to do his sleeping in the winter. But the next few months you boys must reverse that rule. Not that you need to deny yourselves abundant rest, but your vigilance should never sleep. Let your concern for the herd be the first and last thought of the day, and then I'll get my beauty sleep this winter. The unforeseen may happen; but I want you to remember that when storms howl the loudest, your Mr. Quince and I will be right around the bend of the creek, with our ear to the ground, the reserves, listening to the good fight you boys are making. Of course you could call the reserves, but you want the glory of the good fighting and the lust of victory, all to yourselves. That's the way I've got you sized up--die rather than show the white feather. Come on, Dell; we're sleeping in the summer."

CHAPTER IX.
A WINTRY CRUCIBLE

The dreaded winter was at hand. Scarcely a day passed but the harbingers of air and sky sounded the warning approach of the forthcoming siege. Great flights of song and game birds, in their migration southward, lent an accent as they twittered by or honked in mid-air, while scurrying clouds and squally weather bore witness of approaching winter.

The tent was struck and stored away. The extra saddle stock was freed for the winter, and located around Hackberry Grove. The three best horses were given a ration of corn, and on Dell's return from the railroad, the cattle were put under herd. The most liberal freedom must be allowed; with the numbers on hand, the term *close* herding would imply grazing the cattle on a section of land, while *loose* herding would mean four or five times that acreage. New routes must be taken daily; the weather would govern the compactness and course of the herd, while a radius of five miles from the corral was a liberal range.

The brothers were somewhat familiar with winter on the plains. Cold was to be expected, but if accompanied by sunshine and a dry atmosphere, there was nothing to fear. A warm, fine day was usually the forerunner of a storm, the approach of which gave little warning, requiring a sleepless vigilance to avoid being taken unaware or at a disadvantage.

The day's work began at sunrise. Cattle are loath to leave a dry bed, and on throwing open the corral gates, it was often necessary to enter and arouse the herd. Thereafter, under normal conditions, it was a matter of pointing, keeping up the drag cattle, allowing the herd to spread and graze, and contracting and relaxing as occasion required. In handling, it was a decided advantage that the little nucleus had known herd restraint, in trailing overland from Texas, and were obedient, at a distance of fifty yards, to the slightest whistle or pressure of a herdsman. Under favorable conditions, the cattle could be depended on to graze until noon, when they were allowed an hour's rest, and the circle homeward was timed so as to reach the corral and water by sunset. The duties of each day were a repetition of the previous one, the moods of the old and younger cattle, sedate and frolicsome, affording the only variety to the monotony of the task.

"Holding these cattle is going to be no trouble at all," said Dell, as they rode homeward, at the end of the first day's herding. "My horse never wet a hair to-day."

"Don't shout before you're out of the woods," replied Joel. "The first of April will be soon enough to count our chickens. To-morrow is only the beginning of December."

"Last year we shucked corn up until Christmas."

"Husking corn is a burnt bridge with me. We're herding cattle this winter. Sit straight in your saddle."

A week of fine weather followed. The boys were kept busy, early and late, with the details of house and stable. A new route each day was taken with the herd, and after penning in the evening, it was a daily occurrence, before bedtime, to walk back to the corral and see that all was secure. Warning of approach and departure, on the part of the boys, either by whistling or singing, was always given the cattle, and the customary grunting of the herd answered for its own contentment. A parting look was given the horses, their forage replenished, and every comfort looked after to the satisfaction of their masters. By nature, horses are distant and slow of any expression of friendship; but an occasional lump of sugar, a biscuit at noon-time, with the present ration of grain, readily brought the winter mounts to a reliance, where they nickered at the approaching footsteps of their riders.

The trust of the boys, in their winter mounts, entitles the latter to a prominent place in the line of defense. Rowdy, Joel's favorite, was a veteran cow horse, dark brown in color, and, under the saddle, restless, with a knowledge of his work that bordered on the human. Dell favored Dog-toe, a chestnut in color, whose best point was a perfect rein, and from experience in roping could halt from any gait on the space of a blanket. The relay horse was named Coyote, a cinnamon-colored mount, Spanish marked in a black stripe down his back, whose limbs were triple-ringed above the knees, or where the body color merged with the black of his legs. Their names had followed them from the trail, one of which was due to color marks, one to disposition, while that of Dell's chestnut was easily traceable, from black marks in his hoofs quartering into toes.

The first storm struck near the middle of December. It was preceded by an ideal day; like the promise of spring, a balmy south wind swept the range, while at night a halo encircled the moon.

"It will storm within three days," said Dell, as the boys strolled up to the corral for a last look at the sleeping cattle. "There are three stars inside the circle around the moon. That's one of Granny Metcalf's signs."

"Well, we'll not depend on signs," replied Joel. "These old granny omens may be all right to hatch chickens by, but not to hold cattle. All advice on that point seems to rely on corn-fed saddle horses and little sleep."

The brothers spent the customary hour at the corral. From the bluff bank which encircled the inclosure, the lads looked down on the contented herd, their possession and their promise; and the tie of man and his beast was accented anew in their youthful hearts.

"Mr. Paul was telling me on one of our rides," said Joel, gazing down on the sleeping herd, "that we know nothing of the human race in an age so remote that it owned no cattle. He says that when the pyramids of Egypt were being built, ours was then an ancient occupation. I love to hear Mr. Paul talk about cattle. Hark!"

The long howl of a wolf to the south was answered by a band to the westward, and echoed back from the north in a single voice, each apparently many miles distant. Animal instinct is usually unerring, and the boys readily recalled the statement of the old trail foreman, that the howling of wolves was an omen of a forthcoming storm.

"Let it come," said Joel, arising and starting homeward. "We'll meet it. Our course to-morrow will be northwest."

It came with little warning. Near the middle of the following afternoon, a noticeable lull in the wind occurred, followed by a leaden horizon on the west and north. The next breeze carried the icy breath of the northwest, and the cattle turned as a single animal. The alert horsemen acted on the instant, and began throwing the cattle into a compact herd. At the time they were fully three miles from the corral, and when less than halfway home, the storm broke in splendid fury. A swirl of snow accompanied the gale, blinding the boys for an instant, but each lad held a point of the herd and the raging elements could be depended on to bring up the rear.

It was no easy victory. The quarter from which the storm came had been anticipated to a fraction. The cattle drifted before its wrath, dropped into the valley just above the corral, where the boys doubled on the outside point, and by the aid of a wing-gate turned the wandering herd into the enclosure. The rear, lashed by the storm, instinctively followed the leaders, and the gates were closed and roped securely.

It was a close call. The lesson came vividly near to the boys. "Hereafter," said Joel, "all signs of a storm must be acted upon. We corraled these cattle by a scratch. Now I know what a winter drift means. A dozen men couldn't turn this herd from the course of to-day's storm. We must hold nearer the corral."

The boys swung into their saddles, and, trusting to their horses, safely reached the stable. A howling night followed; the wind banked the snow against every obstacle, or filled the depressions, even sifting through every crack and crevice in the dug-out. The boys and their mounts were snug within sod walls, the cattle were sheltered in a cove of the creek, and the storm wailed its dirges unheeded.

Dawn broke cold and clear. Sun-dogs flanked the day's harbinger and sunrise found the boys at the corral gate. The cattle lazily responded to their freedom, the course led to the nearest divide, wind-swept of snow, and which after an hour's sun afforded ample grazing for the day. The first storm of the winter had been met, and its one clear lesson lent a dread to any possible successors. The herd in the grip of a storm, cut off from the corral, had a new meaning to the embryo cowmen. The best advice is mere theory until applied, and experience in the practical things of life is not transferable.

The first storm was followed by ideal winter weather until Christmas day. The brothers had planned an extra supper on that occasion, expecting to excuse Dell during the early afternoon for the culinary task, and only requiring his services on corraling the herd at evening. The plan was feasible, the cattle were herd-broke, knew their bed and water, and on the homeward circle all that was required was to direct and time the grazing herd. The occasion had been looked forward to, partly because it was their very own, their first Christmas spread, and partly on account of some delicacies that their sponsor had forced on Dell on parting at the railroad, in anticipation of the day. The bounds of the supper approached a banquet, and the question of appetites to grace the occasion was settled.

The supper was delayed. Not from any fault in the planning, but the weather had not been consulted. The herd had been grazed out on a northwest course for the day, and an hour after noon, almost the time at which Dell was to have been excused, a haze obscured the sun and dropped like a curtain around the horizon. Scurrying clouds appeared, and before the herd could be thrown together and started, a hazy, leaden sky shot up, almost due west, heralding the quarter of the coming storm. The herd sensed the danger and responded to the efforts of the horsemen; but before a mile had been covered, it was enveloped in swirling snow and veering its march with the course of the storm. The eddying snow blinded the boys as to their direction; they supposed they were pointing the cattle into the valley, unaware that the herd had changed its course on the onslaught of the elements. Confidence gave way to uncertainty, and when sufficient time had elapsed to more than have reached the corral, conjecture as to their location became rife. From the moment the storm struck, both boys had bent every energy to point the herd into the valley, but when neither slope nor creek was encountered, the fact asserted itself that they were adrift and at the mercy of the elements.

"We've missed the corral," shouted Dell. "We're lost!"

"Not yet," answered Joel, amid the din of the howling storm. "The creek's to our right. Loosen your rope and we'll beat these leaders into the valley."

The plying of ropes, the shouting of boys, and the pressure of horses merely turned the foremost cattle, when a new contingent forged to the front, impelled onward by the fury of the storm. Again and again the boys plied the fear of ropes and the force of horses, but each effort was futile, as new leaders stepped into the track of the displaced ones, and the course of the herd was sullenly maintained.

The battle was on, and there were no reserves within call. In a crisis like the present, moments drag like hours, and the firing line needed heartening. A knowledge of the country was of no avail, a rod or two was the limit of vision, and the brothers dared not trust each other out of sight. Time moved forward unmeasured, yet amid all Joel Wells remained in possession of a stanch heart and an unbewildered mind. "The creek's to our right," was his battle cry. "Come on; let's turn these lead cattle once more."

Whether it was the forty-ninth or hundredth effort is not on record, but at some point in the good fight, the boys became aware that the cattle were descending a slope--the welcome, southern slope of the Beaver valley! Overhead the storm howled mercilessly, but the shelter of the hillside admitted of veering the herd on its course, until the valley was reached. No knowledge of their location was possible, and all the brothers could do was to cross to the opposite point, and direct the herd against the leeward bank of the creek. Every landmark was lost, with the herd drifting at will.

The first recognition was due to animal instinct. Joel's horse neighed, was answered by Dell's, and with slack rein, the two turned a few rods aside and halted at their stable door. Even then the boys could scarcely identify their home quarters, so enveloped was the dug-out in swirling snow.

"Get some matches," said Joel, refusing to dismount. "There's no halting these cattle short of the second cut-bank, below on the left. Come on; we must try and hold the herd."

The sullen cattle passed on. The halt was only for a moment, when the boys resumed their positions on the point and front. Allowing the cattle to move, assured a compact herd, as on every attempt to halt or turn it, the rear forged to the front and furnished new leaders, and in unity lay a hope of holding the drifting cattle.

The lay of the Beaver valley below headquarters was well known. The banks of the creek shifted from a valley on one side, to low, perpendicular bluffs on the other. It was in one of these meanderings of the stream that Joel saw a possible haven, the sheltering cut-bank that he hoped to reach, where refuge might be secured against the raging elements. It lay several miles below the homestead, and if the drifting herd reached the bend before darkness, there was a fighting chance to halt the cattle in a protected nook. The cove in mind was larger than the one in which the corral was built, and if a successful entrance could only be effected--but that was the point.

"This storm is quartering across the valley," said Joel, during a lull, "and if we make the entrance, we'll have to turn the herd on a direct angle from the course of the wind. If the storm veers to the north, it will sweep us out of the valley, with nothing to shelter the cattle this side of the Prairie Dog. It's make that entrance, or abandon the herd, and run the chance of overtaking it."

"We'll rush them," said Dell. "Remember how those men, the day we branded, rushed the cattle into the branding chute."

"They could do things that we wouldn't dare--those were trail men."

"The cattle are just as much afraid of a boy as of a man; they don't know any difference. You point them and I'll rush them. Remember that story Mr. Quince told about a Mexican boy throwing himself across a gateway, and letting a thousand range horses jump over him? You could do that, too, if you had the nerve. Watch me rush them."

It seemed an age before the cut-bank was reached. The meanderings of the creek were not even recognizable, and only an occasional willow could be identified, indicating the location of the present drift. Occasionally the storm thickened or lulled, rendering it impossible to measure the passing time, and the dread of nightfall was intensified. Under such stress, the human mind becomes intensely alert, and every word of warning, every line of advice, urged on the boys by their sponsors, came back in their hour of trial with an applied meaning. This was no dress parade, with the bands playing and horses dancing to the champing of their own bits; no huzzas of admiring throngs greeted this silent, marching column; no love-lit eyes watched their hero or soft hand waved lace or cambric from the border of this parade ground.

A lone hackberry tree was fortunately remembered as growing near the entrance to the bend which formed the pocket. When receiving the cattle from the trail, it was the landmark for dropping the cripples. The tree grew near the right bank of the creek, the wagon trail passed under it, making it a favorite halting place when freighting in supplies. Dell remembered its shade, and taking the lead, groped forward in search of the silent sentinel which stood guard at the gateway of the cove. It was their one hope, and by zigzagging from the creek to any semblance of a road, the entrance to the nook might be identified.

The march of the herd was slow and sullen. The smaller cattle sheltered in the lee of the larger, moving compactly, as if the density of the herd radiated a heat of its own. The saddle horses, southern bred and unacclimated, humped their backs and curled their heads to the knee, indicating, with the closing day, a falling temperature. Suddenly, and as clear as the crack of a rifle, the voice of Dell Wells was heard in the lead:--

"Come on, Joel; here's our hackberry! Here's where the fight is won or lost! Here's where you point them while I rush them! Come quick!"

The brothers shifted positions. It was the real fight of the day. Responding to spur and quirt, the horses sprang like hungry wolves at the cattle, and the gloomy column turned quartering into the eye of the storm. But as on every other attempt to turn or mill the drifting herd, new leaders forged to the front and threatened to carry the drift past the entrance to the pocket. The critical moment had arrived. Dismounting, with a coiled rope in hand, Dell rushed on the volunteer leaders, batting them over the heads, until they whirled into the angling column, awakened from their stupor and panic-stricken from the assault of a boy, who attacked with the ferocity of a fiend, hissing like an adder or crying in the eerie shrill of a hyena in the same breath. It worked like a charm! Its secret lay in the mastery of the human over all things created. Elated by his success, Dell stripped his coat, and with a harmless weapon in each hand, assaulted every contingent of new leaders, striking right and left, throwing his weight against their bodies, and by the magic of his mimic furies forcing them into obedience.

Meanwhile Joel had succeeded in holding the original leaders in line, and within a hundred yards from the turn, the shelter of the bend was reached. The domestic bovine lows for the comfort of his stable, and no sooner had the lead cattle entered the sheltering nook, than their voices arose in joyous lowing, which ran back through the column for the first time since the storm struck. Turning to the support of Dell, the older boy lent his assistance, forcing the angle, until the drag end of the column had passed into the sheltering haven. The fight was won, and to Dell's courage, in the decisive moment, all credit was due. The human is so wondrously constructed and so infinite in variety, that where one of these brothers was timid the other laughed at the storm, and where physical courage was required to assault a sullen herd, the daring of one amazed the other. Cattle are the emblem of innocence and strength, and yet a boy--in spite of all that has been written to the contrary--could dismount in the face of the wildest stampede, and by merely waving a handkerchief split in twain the frenzied onrush of three thousand beeves.

Dell recovered his horse, and the brothers rode back and forth across the mouth of the pocket. The cattle were milling in an endless merry-go-round, contented under the sheltering bluffs, lowing for mates and cronies, while above howled the elements with unrelenting fury.

"We'll have to guard this entrance until the cattle bed down for the night," remarked Joel, on surveying the situation. "I wonder if we could start a fire."

"I'll drop back to the hackberry and see if I can rustle some wood," said Dell, wheeling his horse and following the back trail of the cattle. He returned with an armful of dry twigs, and a fire was soon crackling under the cliff. A lodgment of old driftwood was found below the bend, and as darkness fell in earnest, a cosy fire threw its shadows over the nook.

A patrol was established and the night's vigil begun. The sentinel beat was paced in watches between the boys, the width of the gateway being about two hundred yards. There was no abatement of the storm, and it was hours before all the cattle bedded down. The welfare of the horses was the main concern, and the possibility of reaching home before morning was freely discussed. The instinct of the horses could be relied on to find the way to their stable, but return would be impossible before daybreak. The brothers were so elated over holding the cattle that any personal hardship was endurable, and after a seeming age, a lull in the elements was noticeable and a star shone forth. Joel mounted his horse and rode out of the cove, into the open valley, and on returning announced that the storm had broken and that an attempt to reach home was safe.

Quietly as Arabs, the boys stole away, leaving the cattle to sleep out the night. Once the hackberry was reached, the horses were given free rein, when restraint became necessary to avoid galloping home. The snow crunched underfoot, the mounts snorted their protest at hindrance, vagrant breezes and biting cold cut the riders to the marrow, but on approaching the homestead the reins were shaken out and the horses dashed up to the stable door.

"There's the morning star," observed Joel, as he dismounted.

"If we're going to be cowmen," remarked Dell, glancing at the star as he swung out of the saddle, "hereafter we'll eat our Christmas supper in October."

CHAPTER X.
GOOD FIGHTING

Dawn found the boys in the saddle. A two hours' respite had freshened horses and riders. The morning was crimpy cold, but the horses warmed to the work, and covered the two miles to the bend before the sun even streaked the east. Joel rode a wide circle around the entrance to the cove, in search of cattle tracks in the snow, and on finding that none had offered to leave their shelter, joined his brother at the rekindled fire under the cliff. The cattle were resting contentedly, the fluffy snow underneath having melted from the warmth of their bodies, while the diversity of colors in the herd were blended into one in harmony with the surrounding scene. The cattle had bedded down rather compactly, and their breathing during the night had frosted one another like window glass in a humid atmosphere. It was a freak of the frost, sheening the furry coats with a silver nap, but otherwise inflicting no harm.

The cattle were allowed to rise of their own accord. In the interim of waiting for the sun to flood the cove, the boys were able to get an outline on the drift of the day previous. Both agreed that the herd was fully five miles from the corral when the storm struck, and as it dropped into the valley near the improvements (added to their present location), it had drifted fully eight miles in something like five hours.

"Lucky thing for us that it was a local storm," said Joel, as he hovered over the fire. "Had it struck out of the north we would be on the Prairie Dog this morning with nothing but snowballs for breakfast. Relying on signs did us a heap of good. It was a perfect day, and within thirty minutes we were drifting blindly. It's all easy to figure out in advance, but storms don't come by programme. The only way to hold cattle on these plains in the winter is to put your trust in corn-fed saddle horses, and do your sleeping in the summer."

"I wonder when the next storm will strike," meditated Dell.

"It will come when least expected, or threaten for days and days and never come at all," replied Joel. "There's no use sitting up at night to figure it out. Rouse out the cattle, and I'll point them up the divide."

The sunshine had crept into the bend, arousing the herd, but the cattle preferred its warmth to a frosty breakfast, and stood around in bunches until their joints limbered and urgent appetites sent them forth. In spite of the cold, the sun lent its aid, baring the divides and wind-swept places of snow; and before noon, the cattle fell to feeding so ravenously that the herdsmen relayed each other, and a dinner for boy and horse was enjoyed at headquarters. In the valley the snow lay in drifts, but by holding the cattle on divides and southern slopes, they were grazed to contentment and entered their own corral at the customary hour for penning. Old axes had been left at hand, and the first cutting of ice, to open the water for cattle, occupied the boys for fully an hour, after which they rode home to a well-earned rest.

Three days of zero weather followed. Sun-dogs, brilliant as rainbows and stately as sentinels, flanked the rising sun each morning, after which the cold gradually abated, and a week after, a general thaw and warm winds swept the drifts out of the valley. It was a welcome relief; the cattle recovered rapidly, the horses proved their mettle, while the boys came out more than victors. They were inuring rapidly to their new occupation; every experience was an asset in meeting the next one, while their general fibre was absorbing strength from the wintry trial on the immutable plain.

Only once during the late storm were wolves sighted. Near the evening of the second day, a band of three made its appearance, keeping in the distance, and following up the herd until it was corraled at the regular hour. While opening the ice, the boys had turned their horses loose among the cattle, and on leading them out of the corral, the trio of prowlers had crept up within a hundred yards. With a yell, the boys mounted and made a single dash at them, when the wolves turned, and in their hurried departure fairly threw up a cloud of snow.

"That's what Mr. Quince means by that expression of his, 'running like a scared wolf,'" said Joel, as he reined in old Rowdy.

"When will we put out the poison?" breathlessly inquired Dell, throwing his mount back on his haunches in halting.

"Just as soon as they begin to hang around. Remind me, and we'll look for tracks around the corral in the morning. My, but they were beauties! How I would like to have one of their hides for a foot-rug!"

"The first heavy snow that comes will bring them out of the sand hills," said Dell, as they rode home. "Mr. Paul said that hunger would make them attack cattle. Oh, if we could only poison all three!"

Dell rambled on until they reached the stable. He treated his mind to visions of wealth, and robes, and furry overcoats. The wolves had located the corral, the winter had barely begun, but the boys were aware of the presence of an enemy.

A complete circle of the corral was made the following morning. No tracks were visible, nor were any wolves sighted before thawing weather temporarily released the range from the present wintry grip. A fortnight of ideal winter followed, clear, crisp days and frosty nights, ushering in a general blizzard, which swept the plains from the British possessions to the Rio Grande, and left death and desolation in its pathway. Fortunately its harbingers threw its menace far in advance, affording the brothers ample time to reach the corral, which they did at a late evening hour. The day had been balmy and warm, the cattle came in, gorged from a wide circle over buffalo grass, the younger ones, as if instinctive of the coming storm and in gratitude of the shelter, even kicking up their heels on entering the gates. The boys had ample time to reach headquarters, much in doubt even then whether a storm would strike or pass away in blustering threats.

It began at darkness, with a heavy fall of soft snow. Fully a foot had fallen by bedtime, and at midnight the blizzard struck, howling as if all the demons of night and storm were holding high carnival. Towards morning a creeping cold penetrated the shack, something unknown before, and awoke the boys, shivering in their blankets. It was near their hour for rising, and once a roaring fire warmed up the interior of the room, Joel took a peep without, but closed the door with a shudder.

"It's blowing a hurricane," said he, shivering over the stove. "This is a regular blizzard--those others were only squalls. I doubt if we can reach the stable before daybreak. Those poor cattle--"

The horses were their first concern. As was their usual custom, well in advance of daybreak an attempt was made to reach and feed the saddle stock. It was Joel's task, and fortifying himself against the elements without, he announced himself as ready for the dash. It was less than a dozen rods between shack and stable, and setting a tallow dip in the window for a beacon, he threw open the door and sprang out. He possessed a courage which had heretofore laughed at storms, but within a few seconds after leaving the room, he burst open the door and fell on the bed.

"I'm blinded," he murmured. "Put out the light and throw a blanket over my head. The sifting snow cut my eyes like sand. I'll come around in a little while."

Daybreak revealed nothing worse from the driving snow than inflamed eyes and roughened cheeks, when another attempt was made to succor the horses. Both boys joined in the hazard, lashing themselves together with a long rope, and reached the stable in safety. On returning, Dell was thrown several times by the buffeting wind, but recovered his feet, and, following the rope, the dug-out was safely reached.

"That's what happened to me in the darkness," said Joel, once the shelter of the house was reached. "I got whipped off my feet, lost my bearings, and every time I looked for the light, my eyes filled with snow."

There was no abatement of the blizzard by noon. It was impossible to succor the cattle, but the boys were anxious to reach the corral, which was fully a mile from the shack. Every foot of the creek was known, and by hugging the leeward bank some little protection would be afforded and the stream would lead to the cattle. Near the middle of the afternoon, there was a noticeable abatement in the swirling snow, when the horses were blanketed to the limit and an effort made to reach the corral. By riding bareback it was believed any drifts could be forced, at least allowing a freedom to the mounts returning, in case the boys lost their course.

The blizzard blew directly from the north, and crossing the creek on a direct angle, Joel led the way, forcing drifts or dismounting and trampling them out until a pathway was made. Several times they were able to make a short dash between known points, and by hugging the sheltering bank of the creek, safely reached the corral. The cattle were slowly milling about, not from any excitement, the exercise being merely voluntary and affording warmth. The boys fell to opening up the water, the cattle crowding around each opening and drinking to their contentment. An immense comb of snow hung in a semicircle around the bend, in places thirty feet high and perpendicular, while in others it concaved away into recesses and vaults as fantastic as frosting on a window. It was formed from the early, softer snow, frozen into place, while the present shifting frost poured over the comb into the sheltered cove, misty as bride's veiling, and softening the grotesque background to a tint equaled only in the fluffy whiteness of swan's-down.

The corral met every requirement. Its protecting banks sheltered the herd from the raging blizzard; the season had inured the cattle, given them shaggy coats to withstand the cold, and only food was lacking in the present trial. After rendering every assistance possible, the boys remained at the corral, hoping the sun would burst forth at evening, only to meet disappointment, when their horses were given free rein and carried them home in a short, sure dash.

A skirmish for grazing ensued. During the next few days there was little or no sunshine to strip the divides of snow, but the cattle were taken out and given every possible chance. The first noticeable abatement of the storm was at evening of the third day, followed by a diminishing fourth, when for the first time the herd was grazed to surfeiting. The weather gradually faired off, the cattle were recovering their old form, when a freak of winter occurred. A week from the night the blizzard swept down from the north, soft winds crept up the valley, promising thawing weather as a relief to the recent wintry siege. But dawn came with a heavy snow, covering the range, ending in rain, followed by a freezing night, when the snow crusted to carry the weight of a man, and hill and valley lay in the grip of sleet and ice.

It was the unforeseen in the lines of intrenchment. The emergency admitted of no dallying. Cattle do not paw away obstacles as do horses and other animals to reach the grass, and relief must come in the form of human assistance. Even the horses were helpless, as the snow was too deep under the sleet, and any attempt to trample out pathways would have left the winter mounts bleeding and crippled. The emergency demanded men, but two boys came to the front in a resourceful manner. In their old home in Ohio, threshing flails were sometimes used, and within an hour after daybreak Joel Wells had fashioned two and was breaking a trail through the sleet to the corral.

The nearest divide lay fully a mile to the north. To reach it with the cattle, a trail, a rod or more in width, would have to be broken out. Leaving their horses at the corral, the brothers fell at the task as if it had been a threshing floor, and their flails rang out from contact with the icy sleet. By the time they had reached the divide it was high noon, and the boys were wearied by the morning task. The crusted snow lay fully six inches deep on an average, and if sustenance was rendered the cattle, whose hungry lowing reached equally hungry boys, the icy crust must be broken over the feeding grounds.

It looked like an impossible task. "Help me break out a few acres," said Joel, "and then you can go back and turn out the cattle. Point them up the broken-out trail, and bring my horse and come on ahead of the herd. If we can break out a hundred acres, even, the cattle can nose around and get down to the grass. It's our one hope."

The hungry cattle eagerly followed up the icy lane. By breaking out the shallow snow, the ground was made passably available to the feeding herd, which followed the boys as sheep follow a shepherd. Fortunately the weather was clear and cold, and if temporary assistance could be rendered the cattle, a few days' sunshine would bare the ground on southern slopes and around broken places, affording ample grazing. The flails rung until sunset, the sleet was shattered by acres, and the cattle led home, if not sufficiently grazed, at least with hunger stayed.

An inch of soft snow fell the following night, and it adhered where falling, thus protecting the sleet. On the boys reaching the corrals at an unusually early hour, a new menace threatened. The cattle were aroused, milling excitedly in a compact mass, while outside the inclosure the ground was fairly littered with wolf tracks. The herd, already weakened by the severity of the winter, had been held under a nervous strain for unknown hours, or until its assailants had departed with the dawn. The pendulum had swung to an evil extreme; the sleet afforded splendid footing to the wolves and denied the cattle their daily food.

"Shall we put out poison to-night?" inquired Dell, on summing up the situation.

"There's no open water," replied the older boy, "and to make a dose of poison effective, it requires a drink. The bait is to be placed near running water--those were the orders. We've got five hundred cattle here to succor first. Open the gates."

The second day's work in the sleet proved more effective. The sun scattered both snow and ice; southern slopes bared, trails were beaten out to every foot of open ground, and by the middle of the afternoon fully a thousand acres lay bare, inviting the herd to feast to its heart's content. But a night on their feet had tired out the cattle, and it was with difficulty that they were prevented from lying down in preference to grazing. On such occasions, the boys threw aside their flails, and, mounting their horses, aroused the exhausted animals, shifting them to better grazing and holding them on their feet.

"This is the first time I ever saw cattle too tired to eat," said Joel, as the corral gates were being roped shut. "Something must be done. Rest seems as needful as food. This is worse than any storm yet. Half of them are lying down already. We must build a bonfire to-night. Wolves are afraid of a fire."

Fully half the cattle refused to drink, preferring rest or having eaten snow to satisfy their thirst. The condition of the herd was alarming, not from want of food, but from the hungry prowlers of the night. Before leaving, the brothers built a little fire outside the gate, as best they could from the fuel at hand, expecting to return later and replenish the wood supply from headquarters.

The boys were apt in adopting Texas methods. Once the horses were fed and their own supper eaten, the lads fastened onto two dry logs, and from pommels dragged them up to the tiny blaze at the corral opening. It was early in the evening, the herd was at rest, and the light of the bonfire soon lit up the corral and threw fancy shadows on the combing snow which formed the upper rim. The night was crimping cold, and at a late hour the boys replenished the fire and returned home. But as they dismounted at the stable, the hunting cry of a wolf pack was wafted down the valley on the frosty air, and answered by a band far to the south in the sand hills.

"They're coming again," said Joel, breathlessly listening for the distant howling to repeat. "The fire ought to hold them at a distance until nearly morning. Let's feed the horses and turn in for the night."

Daybreak found the boys at the corral. No wolves were in sight, but on every hand abundant evidence of their presence during the night was to be seen. Nearly all the cattle were resting, while the remainder, principally mother cows, were arrayed in battle form, fronting one of the recesses under the combing rim of snow. On riding within the corral, the dread of the excited cows proved to be a monster wolf, crouching on a shelf of snow. He arose on his haunches and faced the horsemen, revealing his fangs, while his breast was covered with tiny icicles, caused by the driveling slaver during the night's run. His weight was responsible for his present plight, he having ventured out on the fragile comb of snow above, causing it to cave down; and in the bewilderment of the moment he had skurried to the safety of the ledge on which he then rested.

It was a moment of excitement. A steady fire of questions and answers passed between the younger and older brother. The wolf was in hand, the horns of a hundred angry cows held the enemy prisoner, and yet the boys were powerless to make the kill. The situation was tantalizing.

"Can't we poison him?" inquired Dell, in the extremity of the moment.

"Certainly. Hand it to him on a plate--with sugar on it."

"If Mr. Paul had only left us his pistol," meditated Dell, as a possibility.

"Yes, you could about hit that bank with a six-shooter. It's the risk of a man's life to wound that wolf. He's cornered. I wouldn't dismount within twenty feet of him for this herd."

"I could shoot him from Dog-toe. This is the horse from which Mr. Paul killed the beef. All trail horses are gun-proof."

"My, but you are full of happy ideas. We've got to let that wolf go--we can't make the kill."

"I have it!" shouted Dell, ignoring all rebuffs. "Dog-toe is a roping horse. Throw wide the gates. Give me a clear field, and I'll lasso that wolf and drag him to death, or wrap him to the centre gatepost and you can kill him with a fence-stay. Dog-toe, I'm going to rope a wolf from your back," added Dell, patting the horse's neck and turning back to the gate. "Show me the mettle of the State that bred you."

"You're crazy," said Joel, "but there's no harm in trying it. Whatever happens, stick to your saddle. Cut the rope if it comes to a pinch. I'll get a fence-stay."

Ever since the killing of the beef, Dell had diligently practiced with a rope. It responded to the cunning of his hand, and the danger of the present moment surely admitted of no false calculations. Dell dismounted with a splendid assurance, tightened the cinches, tied his rope good and firm to the fork of the saddle tree, mounted, and announced himself as ready. The cattle were drifted left and right, opening a lane across the corral, and Dell rode forward to study the situation. Joel took up a position at the gate, armed only with a heavy stay, and awaited the working out of the experiment.

The hazard savored more of inexperience than of courage. Dell rode carelessly back and forth, edging in nearer the ledge each time, whirling his loop in passing, at which the cowering animal arose in an attitude of defense. Nodding to Joel that the moment had come, as the horse advanced and the enemy came within reach, the singing noose shot out, the wolf arose as if to spring, and the next instant Dog-toe whirled under spur and quirt, leaving only a blur behind as he shot across the corral. Only his rider had seen the noose fall true, the taut rope bespoke its own burden, and there was no time to shout. For an instant, Joel held his breath, only catching a swerve in the oncoming horse, whose rider bore down on the centre post of the double gate, the deviation of course being calculated to entangle the rope's victim. The horse flashed through the gate, something snapped, the rope stood in air, and a dull thud was heard in the bewilderment of the moment. The blur passed in an instant, and a monster dog wolf lay at the gatepost, relaxing in a spasm of death.

Dell checked his horse and returned, lamenting the loss of a foot's length from his favorite rope. It had cut on the saddle tree, and thus saved horse and rider from an ugly fall.

"He lays right where I figured to kill him--against that post," said Dell, as he reined in and looked down on the dead wolf. "Do you want his hide, or can I have it?"

"Drag him aside," replied Joel, "while I rouse out the cattle. I'll have to sit up with you to-night."

CHAPTER XI.
HOLDING THE FORT

The valley lay in the grasp of winter. On the hills and sunny slopes, the range was slowly opening to the sun. The creek, under cover of ice and snow, forced its way, only yielding to axes for the time being and closing over when not in use.

The cattle required no herding. The chief concern of the brothers was to open more grazing ground, and to that end every energy was bent. The range already opened lay to the north of the Beaver, and although double the distance, an effort was made to break out a trail to the divide on the south. The herd was turned up the lane for the day, and taking their flails, the boys began an attack on the sleet. It was no easy task, as it was fully two miles to the divide, a northern slope, and not affected by the sun before high noon.

The flails rang out merrily. From time to time the horses were brought forward, their weight shattering the broken sleet and assisting in breaking out a pathway. The trail was beaten ten feet in width on an average, and by early noon the divide was reached. Several thousand acres lay bare, and by breaking out all drifts and depressions running north and south across the watershed, new grazing grounds could be added daily.

A discovery was made on the return trip. The horses had been brought along to ride home on, but in testing the sleet on the divide, the sun had softened the crust until it would break under the weight of either of the boys. By walking well outside the trail, the sleet crushed to the extent of five or six feet, and by leading their horses, the pathway was easily doubled in width. Often the crust cracked to an unknown distance, easing from the frost, which the boys accepted as the forerunner of thawing weather.

"We'll put out poison to-night," said Dell. "It will hardly freeze a shoal, and I've found one below the corral."

"I'm just as anxious as you to put out the bait," replied Joel, "but we must take no chances of making our work sure. The moment the cattle quit drinking, the water holes freeze over. This is regular old Billy Winter."

"I'll show you the ripple and leave it to you," argued the younger boy. "Under this crust of sleet and snow, running water won't freeze."

"Along about sunset we can tell more about the weather for to-night," said Joel, with a finality which disposed of the matter for the present.

On reaching the corral, the older boy was delighted with the splendid trail broken out, but Dell rode in search of a known shallow in the creek. An old wood road crossed on the pebbly shoal, and forcing his horse to feel his way through the softened crust, a riplet was unearthed as it purled from under an earthen bank.

"Here's your running water," shouted Dell, dropping the reins and allowing Dog-toe to drink. "Here you are--come and see for yourself."

Joel was delighted with Dell's discovery. In fact, the water, after emerging from under a concave bank, within a few feet passed under another arch, its motion preventing freezing.

"Don't dismount," said Joel, emphasizing caution, "but let the horses break a narrow trail across the water. This is perfect. We'll build another fire to-night, and lay a half dozen baits around this open water."

The pelt of the dead wolf was taken, when the boys cantered in home. Time was barely allowed to bolt a meal, when the loading of the wooden troughs was begun. Every caution urged was observed; the basins were handled with a hay fork, sledded to the scene, and dropped from horseback, untouched by a human hand. To make sure that the poison would be found, a rope was noosed to the carcass and a scented trace was made from every quarter, converging at the open water and tempting baits.

"There," said Dell, on completing the spoor, "if that doesn't get a wolf, then our work wasn't cunningly done."

"Now, don't forget to throw that carcass back on the ledge, under the comb," added Joel. "Wolves have a reputation of licking each other's bones, and we must deny them everything eatable except poisoned suet."

The herd would not return of its own accord, and must be brought in to the corral. As the boys neared the divide and came in sight of the cattle, they presented a state of alarm. The presence of wolves was at once suspected, and dashing up at a free gallop, the lads arrived in time to save the life of a young steer. The animal had grazed beyond the limits of the herd, unconscious of the presence of a lurking band of wolves, until attacked by the hungry pack. Nothing but the energetic use of his horns saved his life, as he dared not run for fear of being dragged down, and could only stand and fight.

The first glimpse of the situation brought the boys to the steer's rescue. Shaking out their horses, with a shout and clatter of hoofs, they bore down on the struggle, when the wolves suddenly forsook their victim and slunk away. The band numbered eight by easy count, as they halted within two hundred yards and lay down, lolling their tongues as if they expected to return and renew the attack.

"Did you ever hear of anything like this?" exclaimed Dell, as the brothers reined in their horses to a halt. "Attacking in broad daylight!"

"They're starving," replied Joel. "This sleet makes it impossible to get food elsewhere. One of us must stay with the cattle hereafter."

"Well, we saved a steer and got a wolf to-day," boastfully said Dell. "That's not a bad beginning."

"Yes, but it's the end I dread. If this weather lasts a month longer, some of these cattle will feed the wolves."

There was prophecy in Joel's remark. The rescued animal was turned into the herd and the cattle started homeward. At a distance, the wolves followed, peeping over the divide as the herd turned down the pathway leading to the corral. Fuel had been sledded up, and after attending to the details of water and fire, the boys hurried home.

The weather was a constant topic. It became the first concern of the morning and the last observation of the night. The slightest change was noticeable and its portent dreaded. Following the blizzard, every moderation of the temperature brought more snow or sleet. Unless a general thaw came to the relief of the cattle, any change in the weather was undesirable.

A sleepless night followed. It was later than usual when the boys replenished the fire and left the corral. Dell's imagination covered the limits of all possibilities. He counted the victims of the poison for the night, estimated the number of wolves tributary to the Beaver, counted his bales of peltry, and awoke with a start. Day was breaking, the horses were already fed, and he was impatient for saddles and away.

"How many do you say?" insisted Dell, as they left the stable.

"One," answered Joel.

"Oh, we surely got seven out of those eight."

"There were only six baits. You had better scale down your estimate. Leave a few for luck."

Nothing but the cold facts could shake Dell's count of the chickens. Joel intentionally delayed the start, loitering between house and corral, and when no longer able to restrain his impulsive brother, together they reached the scene. Dell's heart failed him--not a dead wolf lay in sight. Every bait had been disturbed. Some of the troughs had been gnawed to splinters, every trace of the poisoned suet had been licked out of the auger holes, while the snow was littered with wolf tracks.

"Our cunning must be at fault," remarked Joel, as he surveyed the scene and empty basins.

Dell looked beaten. "My idea is that we had too few baits for the number of visitors. See the fur, where they fought over the tallow. That's it; there wasn't enough suet to leave a good taste in each one's mouth. From the looks of the ground, there might have been fifty wolves."

The boy reasoned well. Experience is a great school. The brothers awoke to the fact that in the best laid plans of mice and men the unforeseen is ever present. Their sponsors could only lay down the general rule, and the exceptions threw no foreshadows. No one could foresee that the grip of winter would concentrate and bring down on the little herd the hungry, roving wolf packs.

"Take out the herd to-day," said Dell, "and let me break out more running water. I'll take these basins in and refill them, make new ones, and to-night we'll put out fifty baits."

The cattle were pointed up the new trail to the southern divide. Joel took the herd, and Dell searched the creek for other shallows tributary to the corral. Three more were found within easy distance, when the troughs were gathered with fork and sled, and taken home to be refilled. It was Dell Wells's busy day. Cunning and caution were his helpers; slighting nothing, ever crafty on the side of safety, he cut, bored, and charred new basins, to double the original number. After loading, for fear of any human taint, he dipped the troughs in water and laid them in the shade to freeze. A second trip with the sled was required to transport the basins up to the corral, the day's work being barely finished in time for him to assist in penning the herd.

"How many baits have you?" was Joel's hail.

"Sixty odd."

"You'll need them. Three separate wolf packs lay in sight all the afternoon. Several times they crept up within one hundred yards of the cattle. One band numbered upwards of twenty."

"Let them come," defiantly said Dell. "The banquet is spread. Everything's done, except to drag the carcass, and I didn't want to do that until after the cattle were corraled."

The last detail of the day was to build a little fire, which would die out within an hour after darkness. It would allow the cattle time to bed down and the packs to gather. As usual, it was not the intention of the boys to return, and as they mounted their horses to leave, all the welled-up savage in Dell seemed to burst forth.

"Welcome, Mr. Wolf, welcome," said he, with mimic sarcasm and a gesture which swept the plain. "I've worked like a dog all day and the feast is ready. Mrs. Wolf, will you have a hackberry plate, or do you prefer the scent of cottonwood? You'll find the tender, juicy kidney suet in the ash platters. Each table seats sixteen, with fresh water right at hand. Now, have pallets and enjoy yourselves. Make a night of it. Eat, drink, and be merry, for to-morrow your pelts are mine."

"Don't count your chickens too soon," urged Joel.

"To-morrow you're mine!" repeated Dell, ignoring all advice. "I'll carpet the dug-out with your hides, or sell them to a tin peddler."

"You counted before they were hatched this morning," admonished his brother. "You're only entitled to one guess."

"Unless they got enough to sicken them last night," answered Dell with emphasis, "nothing short of range count will satisfy me."

A night of conjecture brought a morning with results. Breakfast was forgotten, saddles were dispensed with, while the horses, as they covered the mile at a gallop, seemed to catch the frenzy of expectation. Dell led the way, ignoring all counsel, until Dog-toe, on rounding a curve, shied at a dead wolf in the trail, almost unhorsing his rider.

"There's one!" shouted Dell, as he regained his poise. "I'll point them out and you count. There's another! There's two more!"

It was a ghastly revel. Like sheaves in a harvest field, dead wolves lay around every open water. Some barely turned from the creek and fell, others struggled for a moment, while a few blindly wandered away for short distances. The poison had worked to a nicety; when the victims were collected, by actual count they numbered twenty-eight. It was a victory to justify shouting, but the gruesome sight awed the brothers into silence. Hunger had driven the enemy to their own death, and the triumph of the moment at least touched one sensitive heart.

"This is more than we bargained for," remarked Joel in a subdued voice, after surveying the ravages of poison.

"Our task is to hold these cattle," replied Dell. "We're soldiering this winter, and our one duty is to hold the fort. What would Mr. Paul say if we let the wolves kill our cattle?"

After breakfast Joel again led the herd south for the day, leaving Dell at the corral. An examination of the basins was made, revealing the fact that every trace of the poisoned suet had been licked out of the holders. Of a necessity, no truce with the wolf became the slogan of the present campaign. No mushy sentiment was admissible--the fighting was not over, and the powder must be kept dry. The troughs were accordingly sledded into the corral, where any taint from the cattle would further disarm suspicion, and left for future use.

The taking of so many pelts looked like an impossible task for a boy. But Dell recalled, among the many experiences with which Forrest, when a cripple, regaled his nurses, was the skinning of winter-killed cattle with a team. The same principle applied in pelting a wolf, where by very little aid of a knife, about the head and legs, a horse could do the work of a dozen men. The corral fence afforded the ready snubbing-post, Dog-toe could pull his own weight on a rope from a saddle pommel, and theory, when reduced to the practical, is a welcome auxiliary. The head once bared, the carcass was snubbed to the centre gate post, when a gentle pull from a saddle horse, aided by a few strokes of a knife, a second pull, and the pelt was perfectly taken. It required steady mounting and dismounting, a gentle, easy pull, a few inches or a foot, and with the patience of a butcher's son, Dog-toe earned his corn and his master a bale of peltry.

Evening brought report of further annoyance of wolves. New packs had evidently joined forces with the remnants of the day before, as there was neither reduction in numbers nor lessening in approach or attitude.

"Ours are the only cattle between the Republican River in Nebraska and the Smoky River in this State," said Joel, in explanation. "Rabbits and other rodents are at home under this sleet, and what is there to live on but stock? You have to hold the cattle under the closest possible herd to avoid attack."

"That will made the fighting all the better," gloatingly declared Dell. "Dog-toe and I are in the fur business. Let the wolves lick the bones of their brethren to-night, and to-morrow I'll spread another banquet."

The few days' moderation in the weather brought a heavy snowfall that night. Fortunately the herd had enjoyed two days' grazing, but every additional storm had a tendency to weaken the cattle, until it appeared an open question whether they would fall a prey to the wolves or succumb to the elements. A week of cruel winter followed the local storm, during which three head of cattle, cripples which had not fully recuperated, in the daily march to the divides fell in the struggle for sustenance and fed the wintry scavengers. It was a repetition of the age-old struggle for existence--the clash between the forces of good and evil, with the wolf in the ascendant.

The first night which would admit of open water, thirty-one wolves fell in the grip of poison. It was give and take thereafter, not an eye for an eye, but in a ratio of ten to one. The dug-out looked like a trapper's cave, carpeted with peltry, while every trace of sentiment for the enemy, in the wintry trial which followed, died out in the hearts of the boys.

Week after week passed, with the elements allied with the wolves against the life of the herd. On the other hand, a sleepless vigilance and sullen resolve on the part of the besieged, aided by fire and poison, alone held the fighting line. To see their cattle fall to feed the wolves, helpless to relieve, was a bitter cup to the struggling boys.

A single incident broke the monotony of the daily grind. One morning near the end of the fifth week, when the boys rode to the corral at an early hour, in order to learn the result of poison, a light kill of wolves lay in sight around the open water. While they were attempting to make a rough count of the dead from horseback, a wolf, supposed to be poisoned, sprang fully six feet into the air, snapping left and right before falling to the ground. Nothing but the agility of Rowdy saved himself or rider, who was nearly unhorsed, from being maimed or killed from the vicious, instant assault.

The brothers withdrew to a point of safety. Joel was blanched to the color of the snow, his horse trembled in every muscle, but Dell shook out his rope.

"Hold on," urged Joel, gasping for breath. "Hold on. That's a mad wolf, or else it's dying."

"He's poisoned," replied Dell. "See how he lays his head back on his flank. It's the griping of the poison. Half of them die in just that position. I'm going to rope and drag him to death."

But the crunching of the horse's feet in the snow aroused the victim, and he again sprang wildly upward, snapping as before, and revealing fangs that bespoke danger. Struggling to its feet, the wolf ran aimlessly in a circle, gradually enlarging until it struck a strand of wire in the corral fence, the rebound of which threw the animal flat, when it again curled its head backward and lay quiet.

"Rope it," said Joel firmly, shaking out his own lasso. "If it gets into that corral it will kill a dozen cattle. That I've got a live horse under me this minute is because that wolf missed Rowdy's neck by a hand-breadth."

The trampled condition of the snow around the corral favored approach. Dell made a long but perfect throw, the wolf springing as the rope settled, closing with one foot through the loop. The rope was cautiously wrapped to the pommel, could be freed in an instant, and whirling Dog-toe, his rider reined the horse out over the lane leading to the herd's feeding ground to the south. The first quarter of a mile was an indistinct blur, out of which a horse might be seen, then a boy, or a wolf arose on wings and soared for an instant. Suddenly the horse doubled back over the lane, and as his rider shot past Joel, a fire of requests was vaguely heard, regarding "a noose that had settled foul," of "a rope that was being gnawed" and a general inability to strangle a wolf.

Joel saw the situation in an instant. The rope had tightened around the wolf's chest, leaving its breathing unaffected, while a few effectual snaps of those terrible teeth would sever any lasso. Shaking out a loop in his own rope, as Dell circled back over the other trail, Rowdy carried his rider within easy casting distance, the lasso hissed through the air, settled true, when two cow-horses threw their weight against each other, and the wolf's neck was broken as easily as a rotten thread.

"A little of this goes a long way with me," said Joel from the safety of his saddle.

"Oh, it's fine practice," protested Dell, as he dismounted and kicked the dead wolf. "Did you notice my throw? If it was an inch, it was thirty feet!"

In its severity, the winter of 1885-86 stands alone in range cattle history. It came rather early, but proved to be the pivotal trial in the lives of Dell and Joel Wells. Six weeks, plus three days, after the worst blizzard in the history of the range industry, the siege was lifted and the Beaver valley groaned in her gladness. Sleet cracks ran for miles, every pool in the creek threw off its icy gorge, and the plain again smiled within her own limits. Had the brothers been thorough plainsmen, they could have foretold the coming thaw, as three days before its harbingers reached them every lurking wolf, not from fear of poison, but instinctive of open country elsewhere, forsook the Beaver, not to return the remainder of the winter.

"That's another time you counted the chickens too soon," said Joel to his brother, when the usual number of baits failed to bring down a wolf.

"Very good," replied Dell. "The way accounts stand, we lost twelve cattle against one hundred and eighteen pelts taken. I'll play that game all winter."

CHAPTER XII.
A WINTER DRIFT

The month of March was the last intrenchment in the wintry siege. If it could be weathered, victory would crown the first good fight of the boys, rewarding their courage in the present struggle and fortifying against future ones. The brothers had cast their lot with the plains, the occupation had almost forced itself on them, and having tasted the spice of battle, they buckled on their armor and rode forth. Without struggle or contest, the worthy pleasures of life lose their nectar.

The general thaw came as a welcome relief. The cattle had gradually weakened, a round dozen had fallen in sacrifice to the elements, and steps must be taken to recuperate the herd.

"We must loose-herd hereafter," said Joel, rejoicing in the thawing weather. "A few warm days and the corral will get miry. Unless the wolves return, we'll not pen the cattle again."

Dell was in high feather. "The winter's over," said he. "Listen to the creek talking to itself. No, we'll not have to corral the herd any longer. Wasn't we lucky not to have any more cattle winter-killed! Every day during the last month I felt that another week of winter would take half the herd. It was good fighting, and I feel like shouting."

"It was the long distance between the corral and the divides that weakened the cattle," said Joel. "Hereafter we'll give them all the range they need and only put them under close-herd at night. There may be squally weather yet, but little danger of a general storm. After this thaw, farmers on the Solomon will begin their spring ploughing."

A fortnight of fine weather followed. The herd was given almost absolute freedom, scattering for miles during the day, and only thrown together at nightfall. Even then, as the cattle grazed entirely by day, a mile square of dry slope was considered compact enough for the night. The extra horses, which had ranged for the winter around Hackberry Grove, were seen only occasionally and their condition noted. The winter had haired them like llamas, the sleet had worked no hardship, as a horse paws to the grass, and any concern for the outside saddle stock was needless.

The promise of spring almost disarmed the boys. Dell was anxious to know the value of the bales of peltry, and constantly urged his brother for permission to ride to the railroad and inquire.

"What's your hurry?" was Joel's rejoinder. "I haven't shouted yet. I'm not sure that we're out of the woods. Let's win for sure first."

"But we ought to write to Mr. Paul and Mr. Quince," urged the younger boy, by way of a double excuse. "There may be a letter from them at Grinnell now. Let's write to our friends in Texas and tell them that we've won the fight. The spring's here."

"You can go to the station later," replied Joel. "The fur will keep, and we may have quite a spell of winter yet. Don't you remember the old weather proverb, of March coming in like a lion and going out like a lamb? This one came in like a lamb, and we had better keep an eye on it for fear it goes out like a lion. You can go to the railroad in April."

There was wisdom in Joel's random advice. As yet there was no response in the earth to the sun's warmth. The grass was timid and refused to come forth, and only a few foolish crows had reached the shrub and willow along the Beaver, while the absence of other signs of spring carried a warning that the wintry elements might yet arise and roar like a young lion.

The one advantage of the passing days was the general improvement in the herd. The instinct of the cattle led them to the buffalo grass, which grew on the slopes and divides, and with three weeks of fair weather and full freedom the herd as a whole rounded into form, reflecting its tenacity of life and the able handling of its owners.

Within ten days of the close of the month, the weakened lines of intrenchment were again assaulted. The herd was grazing westward, along the first divide south of the Beaver, when a squall struck near the middle of the afternoon. It came without warning, and found the cattle scattered to the limits of loose herding, but under the eyes of two alert horsemen. Their mounts responded to the task, circling the herd on different sides, but before it could be thrown into mobile form and pointed into the Beaver valley, a swirl of soft snow enveloped horses and riders, cattle and landscape. The herd turned its back to the storm, and took up the steady, sullen march of a winter drift. Cut off from the corral by fully five miles, the emergency of the hour must be met, and the brothers rode to dispute the progress of the drifting cattle.

"Where can we turn them?" timidly inquired Dell.

"Unless the range of sand dunes catch us," replied Joel, "nothing short of the brakes of the Prairie Dog will check the cattle. We're out until this storm spends its force."

"Let's beat for the sand hills, then. They lay to our right, and the wolves are gone."

"The storm is from the northwest. If it holds from that quarter, we'll miss the sand dunes by several miles. Then it becomes a question of horseflesh."

"If we miss the sand hills, I'll go back and get a pack horse and overtake you to-morrow. It isn't cold, and Dog-toe can face the storm."

"That's our one hope," admitted Joel. "We've brought these cattle through a hard winter and now we mustn't lose them in a spring squall."

The wind blew a gale. Ten minutes after the storm struck and the cattle turned to drift with it, all knowledge of the quarter of the compass was lost. It was a reasonable allowance that the storm would hold a true course until its wrath was spent, and relying on that slender thread, the boys attempted to veer the herd for the sand hills. By nature cattle are none too gregarious, as only under fear will they flock compactly, and the danger of splitting the herd into wandering contingents must be avoided. On the march which lay before it, its compactness must be maintained, and to turn half the herd into the sand dunes and let the remainder wander adrift was out of the question.

"We'll have to try out the temper of the herd," said Joel. "The cattle are thin, have lost their tallow, and this wind seems to be cutting them to the quick. There's no use in turning the lead unless the swing cattle will follow. It's better to drift until the storm breaks than to split the herd into little bunches."

"Let's try for the sand hills, anyhow," urged Dell. "Turn the leaders ever so slightly, and I'll try and keep the swing cattle in line."

An effort to reach the shelter of the sand dunes was repeatedly made. But on each attempt the wind, at freezing temperature, cut the cattle to the bone, and as drifting was so much more merciful, the brothers chose to abandon the idea of reaching a haven in the sand hills.

"The cattle are too weak," admitted Joel, after repeated efforts. "Turn the leaders and they hump their backs and halt. An hour of this wind would drop them in their tracks. It's drift or die."

"I'll drop back and see how the drag cattle are coming on," suggested Dell, "and if they're in line I might as well start after a pack horse. We're only wearing out our horses in trying to turn this herd."

The efforts to veer the herd had enabled the drag end to easily keep in a compact line, and on Dell's return to the lead, he reported the drifting column less than a quarter mile in length.

"The spirit of the herd is killed," said he; "the cattle can barely hold their heads off the ground. Why, during that Christmas drift, they fought and gored each other at every chance, but to-day they act like lost sheep. They are half dead on their feet."

The herd had been adrift several hours, and as sustenance for man and horse was important, Dell was impatient to reach the Beaver before nightfall.

"If the storm has held true since it struck," said he, "I'll cut it quartering from here to headquarters. That good old corn that Dog-toe has been eating all winter has put the iron into his blood, until he just bows his neck and snorts defiance against this wind and snow."

"Now, don't be too sure," cautioned Joel. "You can't see one hundred yards in this storm, and if you get bewildered, all country looks alike. Trust your horse in any event, and if you strike above or below headquarters, if you keep your head on your shoulders you ought to recognize the creek. Give your horse free rein and he'll take you straight to the stable door. Bring half a sack of corn, some bread and meat, the tent-fly and blankets. Start an hour before daybreak, and you'll find me in the lead of the herd."

The brothers parted for the night. So long as he could ride in their lead, the necessity of holding the cattle was the lodestar that sustained Joel Wells during those lonely hours. There was always the hope that the storm would abate, when the tired cattle would gladly halt and bed down, which promise lightened the passing time. The work was easy to boy and horse; to retard the march of the leaders, that the rear might easily follow, was the task of the night or until relieved.

On the other hand, Dell's self-reliance lacked caution. Secure in his ability to ride a course, day or night, fair or foul weather, he had barely reached the southern slope of the Beaver when darkness fell. The horse was easily quartering the storm, but the pelting snow in the boy's face led him to rein his mount from a true course, with the result that several miles was ridden without reaching any recognizable landmark. A ravine or dry wash was finally encountered, when Dell dismounted. As a matter of precaution, he carried matches, and on striking one, confusion assumed the reign over all caution and advice. He was lost, but contentious to the last ditch. Several times he remounted and allowed his horse free rein, but each time Dog-toe turned into the eye of the storm, then the true course home, and was halted. Reason was abandoned and disorder reigned. An hour was lost, when the confident boy mounted his horse and took up his former course, almost crossing the line of storm on a right angle. A thousand visible forms, creatures of the night and storm, took shape in the bewildered mind of Dell

Wells, and after dismounting and mounting unknown times, he floundered across Beaver Creek fully three miles below headquarters.

The hour was unknown. Still confused, Dell finally appealed to his horse, and within a few minutes Dog-toe was in a road and champing the bits against restraint. The boy dismounted, and a burning match revealed the outlines of a road under the soft snow. The horse was given rein again and took the road like a hound, finally sweeping under a tree, when another halt was made. It was the hackberry at the mouth of the cove, its broken twigs bespoke a fire which Dell had built, and yet the mute witness tree and impatient horse were doubted. And not until Dog-toe halted at the stable door was the boy convinced of his error.

"Dog-toe," said Dell, as he swung out of the saddle, "you forgot more than I ever knew. You told me that I was wrong, and you pled with me like a brother, and I wouldn't listen to you. I wonder if he'll forgive me?" meditated Dell, as he opened the stable door.

The horse hurriedly entered and nickered for his feed. "Yes, you shall have an extra ration of corn," answered his rider. "And if you'll just forgive me this once, the lesson you taught me to-night will never be forgotten."

It proved to be early in the evening--only eight o'clock. Even though the lesson was taught by a dumb animal, it was worth its cost. Before offering to sleep, Dell collected all the articles that were to make up the pack, foddered the horses, set the alarm forward an hour, and sought his blankets for a short rest. Several times the howling of the wind awoke him, and unable to sleep out the night, he arose and built a fire. The necessity of a pack saddle robbed him of his own, and, substituting a blanket, at the appointed hour before dawn he started, with three days' rations for man and horse. The snow had ceased falling, but a raw March wind blew from the northwest, and taking his course with it, he reached the divide at daybreak. A struggling sun gave him a bearing from time to time, the sand dunes were sighted, and angling across the course of the wind, the trail of the herd was picked up in the mushy snow. A bull was overtaken, resting comfortably in a buffalo wallow; three others were passed, feeding with the wind, and finally the sun burst forth, revealing the brakes of the Prairie Dog.

Where the cattle had drifted barely two miles an hour, sustenance was following at a five-mile gait. The trail freshened in the snow, narrowed and broadened, and near the middle of the forenoon the scattered herd was sighted. The long yell of warning was answered only by a tiny smoke-cloud, hanging low over the creek bed, and before Joel was aware of his presence, Dell rode up to the very bank under which the fire was burning.

"How do you like an all-night drift?" shouted Dell. "How do snowballs taste for breakfast?"

"Come under the cliff and unpack," soberly replied Joel. "I hope this is the last lesson in winter herding; I fail to see any romance in it."

The horses were unsaddled and fed. "Give an account of yourself," urged Dell, as the brothers returned to the fire. "How did you make out during the night?"

"I just humped my back like the other cattle and took my medicine," replied Joel. "An Indian dances to keep warm, and I sang. You have no idea how good company cattle are. One big steer laid his ear in Rowdy's flank to warm it. I took him by the horn any number of times and woke him up; he was just staggering along asleep. I talked to all the lead cattle, named them after boys we knew at school, and sometimes they would look up when I called to them. And the queerest thing happened! You remember old Redman, our teacher, back in Ohio. Well, I saw him last night. There was a black two-year-old steer among the lead cattle, and every time I looked at him, I saw old Redman, with his humped shoulder, his pug nose, and his half-shut eyes. It took the storm, the sullen drift, to put that expression in the black steer's face, but it was old Redman. During the two terms of school that he taught, he licked me a score of times, but I dared him to come out of that black steer's face and try it again. He must have heard me, for the little black steer dropped back and never came to the lead again."

"And had you any idea where you were?" inquired Dell, prompted by his own experience.

"I was right at home in the lead of the herd. The tepee might get lost, but I couldn't. I knew we must strike the Prairie Dog, and the cattle were within half a mile of it when day broke. Once I got my bearings, Rowdy and I turned on the herd and checked the drift."

A late breakfast fortified the boys for the day. It was fully twenty-five miles back to the Beaver, but with the cattle weakened, the horses worn, it was decided to rest a day before starting on the return. During the afternoon, Dell went back and threw in the stragglers, and towards evening all the cattle were put under loose herd and pointed north. The sun had stripped the snow, and a comfortable camp was made under the cliff. Wood was scarce on the Prairie Dog, but the dry, rank stalks of the wild sunflower made a good substitute for fuel, and night settled over human and animal in the full enjoyment of every comfort.

It was a two-days' trip returning. To Rowdy fell the duty of pack horse. He had led the outward march, and was entitled to an easy berth on retreat.

The tarpaulin was folded the full length of the horse's body girth, both saddles being required elsewhere, and the corn and blankets laid within the pack and all lashed securely. The commissary supplies being light, saddle pockets and cantle strings were found sufficient for their transportation.

The start was made at sunrise. The cattle had grazed out several miles the evening before, and in their weakened condition it would require nursing to reach the Beaver. A mile an hour was the pace, nothing like a compact herd or driving was permissible, and the cattle were allowed to feed or rest at their will. Rowdy grazed along the flank, the boys walked as a relief, and near evening or on sighting the dunes, Dell took the pack horse and rode for their shelter, to locate a night camp. The herd never swerved from its course, and after sunset Joel rounded the cattle into compact form and bedded them down for the night. A beacon fire of plum brush led him to the chosen camp, in the sand hills, where supper awaited the brothers.

"Isn't it lucky," said Dell, as he snuggled under the blankets, "that the wolves are gone. Suppose they were here yet, and we had to build fires, or stand guard over the herd to-night, like trail men, could we do it?"

"Certainly. We met the wolves before and held the cattle. You seem to forget that we're not entitled to sleep any in the winter. Be grateful. Thank the wolf and go to sleep."

"See how the dunes loom up in the light of this camp-fire. I wish Mr. Paul could see it."

"More than likely he has camped in the dunes and enjoyed many rousing fires."

Dell's next remark was unanswered. The stars twinkled overhead, the sandman was abroad, curfew sounded through the dunes, and all was quiet.

"Here's where we burn the wagon," said Joel, as he aroused Dell at daybreak. "It's one of Mr. Quince's remarks, but this is the first time we've had a chance to use it. I'll divide the corn into three good feeds, and we'll make it in home for supper. Let's have the whole hummingbird for breakfast, so that when we ride out of this camp, all worth saving will be the coffee pot and frying pan. So long as we hold the cattle, who cares for expense."

The herd was in hand as it left the bed ground. An ideal spring day lent its aid to the snailing cattle. By the middle of the afternoon the watershed had been crossed, and the gradual slope clown to the Beaver was begun. Rowdy forged to the lead, the flanks turned in, the rear pushed forward, and the home-hunger of the herd found expression in loud and continued lowing.

"I must have been mistaken about the spirit of this herd being killed," observed Dell. "When I left you the other day, to go after a pack horse, these cattle looked dead on their feet. I felt sure that we would lose a hundred head, and we haven't lost a hoof."

"We may have a lot to learn yet about cattle," admitted Joel. "I fully expected to see our back track strung with dead animals."

The origin of the herd, with its deeps and moods, is unknown and unwritten. The domesticity of cattle is dateless. As to when the ox first knew his master's crib, history and tradition are dumb. Little wonder that Joel and Dell Wells, with less than a year's experience, failed to fully understand their herd. An incident, similar to the one which provoked the observation of the brothers, may explain those placid depths, the deep tenacity and latent power of the herd.

After delivering its cargo at an army post, an extensive freighting outfit was returning to the supply point. Twelve hundred oxen were employed. On the outward trip, muddy roads were encountered, the wagons were loaded beyond the strength of the teams, and the oxen had arrived at the fort exhausted, spiritless, and faint to falling under their yokes. Many oxen had been abandoned as useless within one hundred miles of the post, thus doubling the work on the others. On the return trip, these scattered oxen, the lame and halt, were gathered to the number of several hundred, and were being driven along at the rear of the wagon train. Each day added to their numbers, until one fourth of all the oxen were being driven loose at the rear of the caravan. One day a boy blindfolded a cripple ox, which took fright and charged among his fellows, bellowing with fear. It was tinder to powder! The loose oxen broke from the herders, tore past the column of wagons, frenzied in voice and action. The drivers lost control of their teams, bedlam reigned, and the entire wagon train joined in the general stampede. Wagons were overturned and reduced to kindling in a moment of the wildest panic. The drivers were glad to escape with their lives and were left at the rear. A cloud of dust merely marked the direction which the oxen had taken. The teams, six to eight yoke each, wrenched their chains, broke the bows, and joined in the onrush. Many of the oxen, still under yoke, were found the next day fifteen miles distant from the scene of the incident, and unapproachable except on horseback. For a month previous to this demonstration of the latent power of cattle, the humane drivers of the wagon train were constantly lamenting that the spirit of their teams was killed.

When within a mile of the Beaver, the herd was turned westward and given its freedom. While drifting down the slope, Rowdy gradually crept far to the lead, and as the brothers left the cattle and bore off homeward, the horse took up a gentle trot, maintaining his lead until the stable was reached.

"Look at the dear old rascal," said Joel, beaming with pride. "That horse knows more than some folks."

"Yes, and if Dog-toe could talk," admitted Dell, stroking his horse's neck, "he could tell a good joke on me. I may tell it myself some day--some time when I want to feel perfectly ashamed of myself."

CHAPTER XIII.
A WELCOME GUEST

The heralds of spring bespoke its early approach. April was ushered in to the songs of birds, the greening valley, and the pollen on the willow. The frost arose, the earth mellowed underfoot, and the creek purled and sang as it hastened along. The cattle played, calves were born, while the horses, in shedding their winter coats, matted the saddle blankets and threw off great tufts of hair where they rolled on the ground.

The marketing of the peltry fell to Joel. Dell met the wagon returning far out on the trail. "The fur market's booming," shouted Joel, on coming within speaking distance. "We'll not know the price for a few weeks. The station agent was only willing to ship them. The storekeeper was anxious to do the same, and advanced me a hundred dollars on the shipment. Wolf skins, prime, are quoted from two to two dollars and a half. And I have a letter from Forrest. The long winter's over! You can shout! G'long, mules!"

During the evening, Dell read Forrest's letter again and again. "Keep busy until the herds arrive," it read. "Enlarge your water supply and plan to acquire more cattle."

"That's our programme," said Joel. "We'll put in two dams between here and the trail. Mr. Quince has never advised us wrong, and he'll explain things when he comes. Once a week will be often enough to ride around the cattle."

An air of activity was at once noticeable around headquarters. The garden was ploughed and planting begun. The fence was repaired around the corn-field, the beaver dams were strengthened, and sites for two other reservoirs were selected. The flow of the creek was ample to fill large tanks, and if the water could be conserved for use during the dry summer months, the cattle-carrying capacity of the ranch could be greatly enlarged. The old beaver dams around headquarters had withstood every drouth, owing to the shade of the willows overhead, the roots of which matted and held the banks intact. Wagon loads of willow slips were accordingly cut for the new dams and the work begun in earnest.

"We'll take the tent and camp at the lower site," announced Joel. "It would waste too much time to go and come. When we build the upper one, we can work from home."

The two tanks were finished within a month. They were built several miles apart, where there was little or no fall in the creek, merely to hold still water in long, deep pools. The willow cuttings were planted along the borders and around the dams, the ends of which were riprapped with stone, and a spillway cut to accommodate any overflow during freshets.

The dams were finished none too soon, as a dry spring followed, and the reservoirs had barely filled when the creek ceased flowing. The unusual winter snowfall had left a season's moisture in the ground, and the grass came in abundance, matting slope and valley, while the garden grew like a rank weed. The corn crop of the year before had repaid well in forage, and was again planted. In the face of another drouthy summer, the brothers sowed as if they fully expected to reap. "Keep busy" was the slogan of the springtime.

The month of June arrived without a sign of life on the trail. Nearly one hundred calves were born to the herd on the Beaver, the peltry had commanded the highest quotation, and Wells Brothers swaggered in their saddles. But still the herds failed to come.

"Let's put up the tent," suggested Dell, "just as if we were expecting company. Mr. Paul or Mr. Quince will surely ride in some of these evenings. Either one will reach here a full day in the lead of his herd. Let's make out that we're looking for them."

Dell's suggestion was acted on. A week passed and not a trail man appeared. "There's something wrong," said Joel, at the end of the second week. "The Lovell herds go through, and there's sixteen of them on the trail."

"They're water-bound," said Dell, jumping at a conclusion.

"Waterbound, your foot! The men and horses and cattle can all swim. Don't you remember Mr. Quince telling about rafting his wagon across swimming rivers? Waterbound, your grandmother! High water is nothing to those trail men."

Dell was silenced. The middle of June came and the herds had not appeared. The brothers were beginning to get uneasy for fear of bad news, when near dark one evening a buckboard drove up. Its rumbling approach hurried the boys outside the tent, when without a word of hail, Quince Forrest sprang from the vehicle, grasped Dell, and the two rolled over and over on the grass.

"I just wanted to roll him in the dirt to make him grow," explained Forrest to an elderly man who accompanied him. "These are my boys. Look at that red-headed rascal--fat as a calf with two mothers. Boys, shake hands with Mr. Lovell."

The drover alighted and greeted the boys with fatherly kindness. He was a frail man, of medium height, nearly sixty years of age, with an energy that pulsed in every word and action. There was a careworn expression in his face, while an intensity of purpose blazed from hungry, deep-set eyes which swept every detail of the scene at a glance. That he was worried to the point of exhaustion was evident the moment that compliments were exchanged.

"Show me your water supply," said he to Joel; "old beaver ponds, if I am correctly informed. We must move fifty thousand cattle from Dodge to the Platte River within the next fortnight. One of the worst drouths in the history of the trail confronts us, and if you can water my cattle between the Prairie Dog and the Republican River, you can name your own price."

"Let's drive around," said Forrest, stepping into the blackboard, "before it gets too dark. Come on, boys, and show Mr. Lovell the water."

All four boarded the vehicle, the boys standing up behind the single seat, and drove away. In a mile's meanderings of the creek were five beaver ponds, over which in many places the willows interlapped. The pools stood bank full, and after sounding them, the quartette turned homeward, satisfied of the abundant water supply.

"There's water and to spare for the entire drive," said Forrest to his employer. "It isn't the amount drank, it's the absorption of the sun that gets away with water. Those willows will protect the pools until the cows come home. I felt sure of the Beaver."

"Now, if we can arrange to water my herds here--"

"That's all arranged," replied Forrest. "I'm a silent partner in this ranch. Anything that Wells Brothers owns is yours for the asking. Am I right, boys?"

"If Mr. Lovell needs the water, he is welcome to it," modestly replied Joel.

"That's my partner talking," said Forrest; "that was old man Joel Wells that just spoke. He's the senior member of the firm. Oh, these boys of mine are cowmen from who laid the rail. They're not out to rob a neighbor. Once you hear from the head of the Stinking Water, you can order the herds to pull out for the Platte."

"Yes," said Mr. Lovell, somewhat perplexed. "Yes, but let's get the water on the Beaver clear first. What does this mean? I offer a man his price to water my cattle, and he answers me that I'm welcome to it for nothing. I'm suspicious of the Greeks when they come bearing gifts. Are you three plotting against me?"

"That's it," replied Forrest. "You caught the gleam of my axe all right. In the worry of this drouth, you've overlooked the fact that you have five horses on this ranch. They were left here last fall, expecting to pick them up this spring. Two of them were cripples and three were good cow horses. Now, these boys of mine are just branching out into cattle, and they don't need money, but a few good horses are better than gold. That's about the plot. What would you say was the right thing to do?"

Mr. Lovell turned to the boys. "The five horses are yours. But I'm still in your debt. Is there anything else that you need?"

The question was repeated to Forrest. "By the time the herds reach here," said he, mildly observant, "there will be quite a number of tenderfooted and fagged cattle. They could never make it through without rest, but by dropping them here, they would have a fighting chance to recuperate before winter. There won't be a cent in an abandoned steer for you, but these boys--"

"Trim the herds here on the Beaver," interrupted Mr. Lovell. "I'll give all my foremen orders to that effect. Cripples are worthless to me, but good as gold to these boys. What else?"

"Oh, just wish the boys good luck, and if it ever so happens, speak a good word for the Wells Brothers. I found them white, and I think you'll find them on the square."

"Well, this is a happy termination," said Mr. Lovell, as he alighted at the tent. "Our water expense between Dodge and Ogalalla will not exceed five thousand dollars. It cost me double that getting out of Texas."

Secure on the Beaver, the brothers were unaware of the outside drouth, which explained the failure of the herds to appear on the trail as in other years. It meant the delay of a fortnight, and the concentration of a year's drive into a more limited space of time. Unconscious of its value, the boys awoke to the fact that they controlled the only water between the Prairie Dog and the Republican River--sixty miles of the plain. Many of the herds were under contract and bond to cattle companies, individuals, army posts, and Indian agencies, and no excuse would be accepted for any failure to deliver. The drouth might prove an ill-wind to some, but the Beaver valley was not only exempt but could extend relief.

After supper, hosts and guests adjourned to the tent. Forrest had unearthed the winter struggle of his protégés, and gloating over the manner in which the boys had met and overcome the unforeseen, he assumed an observant attitude in addressing his employer.

"You must be working a sorry outfit up on the Little Missouri," said he, "to lose ten per cent of straight steer cattle. My boys, here on the Beaver, report a measly loss of twelve head, out of over five hundred cattle. And you must recollect that these were rag-tag and bob-tail, the flotsam of a hundred herds, forty per cent cripples, walking on crutches. Think of it! Two per cent loss, under herd, a sleet over the range for six weeks, against your ten per cent kill on an open range. You must have a slatterly, sore-thumbed lot of men on your beef ranch."

Mr. Lovell was discouraged over the outlook of his cattle interests. "That was a first report that you are quoting from," said he to Forrest. "It was more prophecy than statement. We must make allowances for young men. There is quite a difference between getting scared and being hurt. My beef outfit has orders to go three hundred miles south of our range and cover all round-ups northward. It was a severe winter, and the drift was heavy, but I'm not worrying any about that sore-fingered outfit. Promptly meeting government contracts is our work to-day. My cattle are two weeks behind time, and the beef herds must leave Dodge to-morrow. Help me figure it out: Can you put me on the railroad by noon?" he concluded, turning to Joel.

"Easily, or I can carry a message to-night."

"There's your programme," said Forrest, interceding. "One of these boys can take you to Grinnell in time for the eastbound train. Wire your beef herds to pull out for the Platte. You can trust the water to improve from here north."

"And you?" inquired the drover, addressing his foreman.

"I'll take the buckboard and go north until I meet Paul. That will cover the last link in the trail. We'll know our water then, and time our drives to help the cattle. It's as clear as mud."

"Just about," dubiously answered Mr. Lovell. "Unless I can get an extension of time on my beef contracts, the penalty under my bonds will amount to a fortune."

"The army is just as well aware of this drouth as you are," said Forrest, "and the War Department will make allowances. The government don't expect the impossible."

"Yes," answered the old drover with feeling. "Yes, but it exacts a bond, and stipulates the daily forfeiture, and if any one walks the plank, it's not your dear old Uncle Samuel. And it matters not how much sleep I lose, red tape never worries."

The boys made a movement as if to withdraw, and Forrest arose. "The programme for to-morrow, then, is understood," said the latter. "The horses will be ready at daybreak."

It was midnight when the trio sought their blankets. On the part of the brothers, there was a constant reference to their guest, the drover, and a desire, if in their power, to aid him in every way.

"I wanted you boys to meet and get acquainted with Mr. Lovell," said Forrest, as all were dozing off to sleep. "There is a cowman in a thousand, and his word carries weight in cattle matters. He's rather deep water, unless you cross or surprise him. I nagged him about the men on his beef ranch. He knew the cattle wouldn't winter kill when they could drift, and the round-up will catch every living hoof. He was too foxy to borrow any trouble there, and this long yell about the drouth interfering with delivery dates keeps the trail outfits against the bits. Admitting his figures, the water expense won't be a drop in the bucket. It affords good worrying and that keeps the old man in fighting form. I'm glad he came along; treat him fair and square, and his friendship means something to you, boys."

CHAPTER XIV.
AN ILL WIND

The start to the station was made at four o'clock in the morning. Joel accompanied the drover, the two best horses being under saddle, easily capable of a road gait that would reach the railroad during the early forenoon. The direct course lay across country, and once the sun flooded the Beaver valley, the cowman swung around in the saddle and his practical eye swept the range. On sighting Hackberry Grove, the broken country beyond, including the sand hills, he turned to his guide.

"My boy," said Mr. Lovell, "you brothers have a great future before you. This is an ideal cattle range. The very grass under our horses' feet carries untold wealth. But you lack cattle. You have the range here for thousands where you are running hundreds. Buy young steers; pay any price; but get more cattle. The growth of young steers justifies any outlay. Come down to Dodge about the first of August. This drouth is liable to throw some bargains on that market. Be sure and come. I'll keep an eye open in your interest on any cattle for sale."

The old drover's words bewildered Joel. The ways and means were not entirely clear, but the confidence of the man in the future of the brothers was gratifying. Meanwhile, at the little ranch the team stood in waiting, and before the horseman had passed out of sight to the south the buckboard started on its northern errand. Dell accompanied it, protesting against his absence from home, but Forrest brushed aside every objection.

"Come on, come on," said he to Dell; "you have no saddle, and we may be back to-night. We're liable to meet Paul on the Republican. Turn your ranch loose and let it run itself. Come on; we ain't halfway through our figuring."

Joel returned after dark. Priest had left Ogalalla, to the north, the same day that Forrest and his employer started up the trail from the south, and at the expected point the two foremen met. The report showed water in abundance from the Republican River northward, confirming Forrest's assertion to his employer, and completing the chain of waters between

Dodge and Ogalalla. Priest returned with the buckboard, which reached the Beaver after midnight, and aroused Joel out of heavy sleep.

"I just wanted to say," said Priest, sitting on the edge of Joel's bunk, "that I had my ear to the ground and heard the good fighting. Yes, I heard the sleet cracking. You never saw me, but I was with you the night you drifted to the Prairie Dog. Take it all along the line, wasn't it good fighting?"

"Has Dell told you everything?" inquired Joel, sitting up in his blankets.

"Everything, including the fact that he got lost the night of the March drift, while going home after a pack horse. Wouldn't trust poor old Dog-toe, but run on the rope himself! Landed down the creek here a few miles. News to you? Well, he admits that the horse forgot more than he himself ever knew. That's a hopeful sign. As long as a man hearkens to his horse, there is no danger of bad counsel being thrust on him."

The boys were catching, at first hand, an insight into the exacting nature of trail work. Their friends were up with the dawn, and while harnessing in the team, Forrest called Joel's attention to setting the ranch in order to water the passing herds.

"I was telling Dell yesterday," said he, "the danger of Texas fever among wintered cattle, and you must isolate your little herd until after frost falls. Graze your cattle up around Hackberry Grove, and keep a dead-line fully three miles wide between the wintered and through trail herds. Any new cattle that you pick up, cripples or strays, hold them down the creek--between here and the old trail crossing. For fear of losing them you can't even keep milk cows around the ranch, so turn out your calves. Don't ask me to explain Texas fever. It's one of the mysteries of the trail. The very cattle that impart it after a winter in the north catch the fever and die like sheep. It seems to exist, in a mild form, in through, healthy cattle, but once imparted to native or northern wintered stock, it becomes violent and is usually fatal. The sure, safe course is to fear and avoid it."

The two foremen were off at an early hour. Priest was again in charge of Lovell's lead herd, and leaving the horse that he had ridden to the Republican River in care of the boys, he loitered a moment at parting.

"If my herd left Dodge at noon yesterday," said he, mentally calculating, "I'll overtake it some time to-morrow night. Allowing ten days to reach here--"

He turned to the boys. "This is the sixteenth of June. Well, come out on the divide on the morning of the twenty-fifth and you will see a dust cloud in the south. The long distance between waters will put the herd through on schedule time. Come out and meet me."

The brothers waved the buckboard away. The dragging days were over. The herds were coming, and their own little ranch promised relief to the drover and his cattle.

"Mr. Quince says the usual price for watering trail herds is from one to three cents a head," said Dell, as their friends dipped from sight. "The government, so he says, allows three cents for watering cavalry horses and harness mules. He tells me that the new settlers, in control of the water on the trail, in northern Texas, fairly robbed the drovers this year. The pastoral Texan, he contends, shared his canteen with the wayfarer, and never refused to water cattle. He wants us to pattern after the Texans--to give our water and give it freely. When Mr. Lovell raised the question of arranging to water his herds from our beaver ponds, do you remember how Mr. Quince answered for us? I'm mighty glad money wasn't mentioned. No money could buy Dog-toe from me. And Mr. Lovell gave us three of our best horses."

"He offered me ten dollars for taking him to the railroad," said Joel, "but I looked him square in the eye and refused the money. He says we must buy more cattle. He wants me to come to Dodge in August, and I'm going."

Dell treated the idea of buying cattle with slight disdain. "You--going--to--buy--more--cattle?" said he, accenting each word. "Any one tell your fortune lately?"

"Yes," answered the older boy. "I'm having it told every day. One of those two men, the gray-haired one on that buckboard,--stand here and you can see them,--told me over a year ago that this range had a value, and that we ought to skirmish some cattle, some way, and stock it. What he saw clearly then, I see now, and what Mr. Lovell sees now, you may see a year hence. These men have proved their friendship, and why stand in our own light? Our ability to hold cattle was tested last winter, and if this range is an asset, there may be some way to buy more cattle. I'm going to Dodge in August."

Dell was silenced. There was ample time to set the ranch in order. Turning away from the old trail, on the divide, and angling in to headquarters, and thence northward, was but a slight elbow on the general course of the trail herds. The long distance across to the Republican would compel an early watering on the Beaver, that the cattle might reach the former river the following evening. The brothers knew to a fraction the grazing gait of a herd, the trailing pace, and could anticipate to an hour the time required to move a herd from the Prairie Dog to the Beaver.

The milk cows and calves were turned back into the general herd. The dead-line was drawn safely below Hackberry Grove, between imaginary landmarks on either slope, while on the creek, like a sentinel, stood a lone willow which seemed to say, "Thus far shalt thou go and no farther." The extra horses, now in the pink of condition, were brought home and located below the ranch, and the house stood in order.

The arrival of the first herd had been correctly calculated. The brothers rode out late on the morning designated, but did not reach the divide. The foremost herd was met within seven miles of the Beaver, the leaders coming on with the steady stride of thirsty cattle that had scented water. Priest was nowhere in sight, but the heavy beeves identified the herd, and when the boys hailed a point man, the situation cleared.

"Mr. Paul--our boss?" repeated the point man. "He's setting up a guide-board, back on the divide, where we turned off from the old trail. Say, does this dim wagon track we're following lead to Wells Brothers' ranch?"

"It does," answered Joel. "You can see the willows from the next swell of the prairie," added Dell, as the brothers passed on.

It was a select herd of heavy beeves. In spite of the drouth encountered, the cattle were in fine condition, and as the herd snailed forward at its steady march, the sweep of horn, the variety of color, the neat outline of each animal blended into a pastoral picture of strength and beauty.

The boys rode down the advancing column. A swing man on the opposite side of the herd waved his hand across to the brothers, and while the two were speculating as to who he might be, a swing lad on the left reined out and saluted the boys.

With hand extended, he smilingly inquired, "Don't you remember the day we branded your cattle? How did the Two Bars and the ---- Y cows winter?"

"It's Billy Honeyman," said Dell, beaming. "Who is that man across the herd, waving at us?" he inquired, amid hearty greeting.

"That's Runt Pickett, the little fellow who helped us brand--the lad who rushed the cattle. The herd cuts him off from shaking hands. Turn your horses the other way and tell me how you like it out West."

Dell turned back, but Joel continued on. The column of beeves was fully a mile in length. After passing the drag end of the herd, the wagon and remuda were sighted, later met, with the foreman still at the rear. The dust cloud of yet another herd arose in the distance, and while Joel pondered on its location over the divide, a horseman emerged from a dip in the plain and came toward him in a slow gallop.

"There's no foreman with the next herd," explained Priest, slacking his horse into a walk, "and the segundo wasn't sure which swell was the real divide. We trailed two herds past your ranch last summer, but the frost has mellowed up the soil and the grass has overgrown the paths until every trace is gone. I planted a guide-post and marked it 'Lovell's Trail,' so the other foremen will know where to turn off. All the old man's herds are within three or four days' drive, and after that it's almost a solid column of cattle back to Dodge. Forrest is in charge of the rear herd, and will pick up any of our abandoned cattle."

The two shook out their mounts, passed the commissary and saddle stock, but halted a moment at the drag end of the herd. "We've been dropping our cripples," explained Priest, "but the other herds will bring them through. There's not over one or two here, but I'm going to saw off three horses on Wells Brothers. Good ones, too, that is, good for next year."

A halt was made at the lead of the herd, and some directions given the point man. It was still early in the forenoon, and once man and boy had fairly cleared the leaders in front, a signal was given and the cattle turned as a single animal and fell to grazing. The wagon and remuda never halted; on being joined by the two horsemen, they continued on into the Beaver. Eleven o'clock was the hour named to water the herd, and punctual to the moment the beeves, with a mile-wide front, were grazed up to the creek.

The cattle were held around the pools for an hour. Before dinner was over, the acting foreman of the second herd rode in, and in mimicking a trail boss, issued some drastic orders. The second herd was within sight, refused to graze, and his wagon was pulling in below the ranch for the noon camp.

Priest looked at his watch. "Start the herd," said he to his own men. "Hold a true northward course, and camp twelve miles out to-night. I may not be with you, but water in the Republican at six o'clock to-morrow evening. Bring in your herd, young fellow," he concluded, addressing the segundo.

The watering of a trail herd is important. Mere opportunity to quench thirst is not sufficient. The timid stand in awe of the strong, and the excited milling cattle intimidate the weak and thirsty. An hour is the minimum time, during which half the herd may drink and lie down, affording the others the chance to approach without fear and slake their thirst.

The acting foreman signaled in his herd. The beeves around the water were aroused, and reluctantly grazed out on their course, while the others came on with a sullen stride that thirst enforces. The previous scene of contentment gave way to frenzy. The heavy beeves, equally select with the vanguard, floundered into the pools, lowed in their joy, drank to gorging, fought their fellows, staggered out of the creek, and dropped to rest in the first dust or dry grass.

Priest trimmed his own beeves and remuda. A third herd appeared, when he and the acting foreman culled over both horses and cattle, and sent the second herd on its way. Each of the three advance herds must reach the Republican the following day, and it was scant two o'clock when the third one trailed out from the Beaver. With mature cattle there were few cripples, and the day ended with an addition to the little ranch of the promised horses and a few tender-footed beeves. There were two more herds of heavy beef cattle to follow, which would arrive during the next forenoon, and the old foreman remained over until the last cattle, intended for army delivery, had passed the ranch.

The herd never fails. Faith in cattle is always rewarded. From that far distant dawn when man and his ox started across the ages the one has ever sustained the other. The two rear beef herds promptly reached the Beaver the next morning, slaked their thirst, and passed on before noon.

"This lets me out as your guest," said Priest to the boys, when the last herd was trimmed. "Bob Quirk will now follow with six herds of contract cattle. He's the foreman of the second herd of beeves, but Mr. Lovell detailed him to oversee this next division across to the Platte. Forrest will follow Quirk with the last five herds of young steers, slated for the old man's beef ranch on the Little Missouri. That puts our cattle across the Beaver, but you'll have plenty of company for the next month. Mr. Lovell has made a good talk for you boys around Dodge, and if you'll give these trail drovers this water, it will all come back. As cowmen, there are two things that you want to remember--that it'll rain again, and that the cows will calve in the spring."

Priest had barely left the little ranch when Bob Quirk arrived. Before dismounting, he rode around the pools, signaled in a wagon and remuda, and returned to the tent.

"This is trailing cattle with a vengeance," said he, stripping his saddle from a tired horse. "There has been such a fight for water this year that every foreman seems to think that unless he reaches the river to-day it'll be dry to-morrow. Five miles apart was the limit agreed on before leaving Dodge, and here I am with six herds--twenty thousand cattle!--within twenty miles of the Beaver. For fear of a stampede last night, we threw the herds left and right, two miles off the trail. The Lord surely loves cattle or the earth would have shook from running herds!"

That afternoon and the next morning the second division of the Lovell herds crossed the Beaver. Forrest rode in and saluted the boys with his usual rough caress.

"Saddle up horses," said he, "and drop back and come through with the two rear herds, There's a heavy drag end on each one, and an extra man to nurse those tender cows over here, to home and friends, will be lending a hand to the needy. I'll run the ranch while you're gone. One of you to each, the fourth and fifth herds, remember. I'll meet you to-morrow morning, and we'll cut the cripples out and point them in to the new tanks below. Shake out your fat horses, sweat them up a little--you're needed at the rear of Lovell's main drive."

The boys saddled and rode away in a gallop. Three of the rear herds reached the Beaver that afternoon, watered, and passed on to safe camps beyond. One of Quirk's wagons had left a quarter of beef at headquarters, and Forrest spent the night amid peace and plenty where the year before he lay wounded.

The next morning saw the last of the Lovell herds arrive. The lead one yielded ninety cripples, and an hour later the rear guard disgorged a few over one hundred head. The two contingents were thrown together, the brothers nursed them in to the new tanks, where they were freed on a perfect range. A count of the cripples and fagged cattle, culled back at headquarters, brought the total discard of the sixteen herds up to two hundred and forty-odd, a riffraff of welcome flotsam, running from a young steer to a seven-year-old beef. The sweepings had paid the reckoning.

Several other trail foremen, scouting in advance of their herds, had reached the Beaver, or had been given assurance that water was to be had in abundance. A measurement of the water was awaited with interest, and once the rear herd grazed out from the beaver ponds, Forrest and the brothers rode around the pools to take soundings.

"I cut notches on willow roots, at each beaver dam, and the loss runs from four to six inches, the lower pools suffering the heaviest," said Joel, summing up the situation.

"They're holding like cisterns," exultingly said Forrest. "Fifty thousand cattle watered, and only lowered the pools on an average of five inches. The upper one's still taking water--that's the reason it's standing the drain. Write it in the sand or among the stars, but the water's here for this year's drive. Go back and tell those waiting foremen to bring on their cattle. Headquarters ranch will water every trail herd, or break a tug trying."

CHAPTER XV.
WATER! WATER!

"Bring on your herds," said Joel, addressing a quartette of trail foremen resting under the sunshade. "Our water is holding out better than we expected. The Lovell cattle only lowered the ponds a trifle. From the present outlook, we can water the drive."

"That's a big contract," reluctantly admitted a "Running W" trail boss. "I had word on the railroad yesterday that the Arkansaw River at Dodge was only running at night."

"Water is reported plentiful around Ogalalla and beyond," doggedly said a pock-marked foreman.

"That'll tempt the herds to cross over," urged the Running W man. "The faraway hills are always green."

The conversation took a new tack. "Who knows the estimate on the total drive this year?" inquired a swarthy, sun-burned little man, addressing the pock-marked foreman.

"A rough estimate places the drive at six hundred and fifty thousand head," came the languid reply.

"There you are," smilingly said the Running W boss, turning to Joel. "Better revise your water estimate."

"Not now," answered Joel, meeting smile with smile. "Later on I may have to hedge, but for the present, bring on your cattle."

"That's to the point," languidly said a tall, blond Texan, arising. "My cattle must have water this evening."

The other trail foremen arose. "We all understand," remarked the pock-marked man to the others, "that this is the place where we drop our strays, fagged and crippled stuff. These are the boys that Mr. Lovell mentioned as worthy of any cattle that must be abandoned."

"At Wells Brothers' ranch, on the Beaver," assentingly said the little man.

"Our lead herds will not have many cripples," said the Running W foreman, turning to the boys. "A few days' rest is everything to a tender-footed steer, and what cattle the lead ones drop, the rear ones have orders to bring through to you."

"Thank you, sir," said Joel frankly. "We want to stock our range, and crippled cattle are as good as gold to us."

Spurs clanked as the men turned to their mounts. The boys followed, and Dell overtook the blond Texan. "If you need a hand on the drag end of your herd," said the boy to the tall foreman, "I'll get up a fresh horse and overtake you."

"Make it a horse apiece," said the young man, "and I'll sign your petition for the post office--when this country has one. I'm as good as afoot."

The other foremen mounted their horses. "I'll overtake you," said Joel to the trio, "as soon as I change mounts. Whoever has the lead herd, come in on the water above the field. The upper pools are the deepest, and let your cattle cover the water evenly."

"I'm in the lead," said the pock-marked man. "But we'll have to come up to the water in trailing formation. The cattle have suffered from thirst, and they break into a run at sight of water, if grazed up to it. You may take one point and I'll take the other."

The existing drouth promised a good schooling for the brothers. Among the old philosophies, contact was said to be educational. Wells Brothers were being thrown in contact with the most practical men that the occupation, in all pastoral ages, had produced. The novelty of trailing cattle vast distances had its origin with the Texans. Bred to the calling, they were masters of the craft. In the hands of an adept outfit of a dozen men, a trail herd of three thousand beeves had all the mobility of a brigade of cavalry. The crack of a whip was unheard on the trail. A whispered order, followed by a signal to the men, and the herd turned, grazed to its contentment, fell into column formation, and took up its march--a peaceful march that few armies have equaled. Contact with these men, the rank and file of that splendid cavalry which once patrolled the range industry of the West, was priceless to the boys.

The lead herd reached the Beaver valley at noon. When within a mile of the water, the point men gave way to the foremen and Joel Wells. But instead of dropping back, the dust-covered men rode on into the lead, the action being seemingly understood by every one except the new hand on the point. Joel was alert, felt the massive column of beeves yield to his slightest pressure, as a ship to the hand of the helmsman, as he veered the leaders out of the broken trails and guided the herd around the field to the upper pools. On nearing the water, the deposed point men deployed nearer the lead, when the object of their position explained itself. On sighting the ponds, the leaders broke into a run, but the four horsemen at hand checked the excited dash, and the herd was led up to the water in column formation. It was the mastery of man over the creature.

The herds arrived in hit-and-miss class. The destination of the pock-marked foreman's beeves was an army post in Dakota. The swarthy little man followed with a herd of cows for delivery at an Indian agency in Wyoming. The different Running W herds were under contract to different cattle companies, in adjoining states and territories. The tall foreman's herd was also under contract, but the point of delivery was at Ogalalla, on the Platte, where a ranch outfit would receive the cattle.

The latter herd arrived late at evening. The cattle were driven on speculation, there had been an oversight in mounting the outfit, and the men, including the foreman, were as good as afoot.

"This trip lets me out," said the young Texan to the brothers, "of walking up the trail and leading fagged-out saddle stock. A mount of six horses to the man may be all right on a ranch, but it won't do on the trail. Especially in a dry year, with delivery on the Platte. Actually, this afternoon is the first time I have felt a horse under me since we crossed Red River. Give me a sheet of paper, please. I want to give you a bill of sale for these six drag ponies that I'm sawing off on you. I carry written authority to give a bill of sale, and it will always protect your possession of the horses. They wouldn't bring a dollar a head in Ogalalla, but when they round into form again next summer, some brand ferret passing might want to claim them on you. Any cattle that I cull out here are abandoned, you understand, simply abandoned."

The boys were left alone for the first time in several nights. The rush of the past few days had kept them in the saddle during their waking hours. The dead-line had been neglected, the drifting of cripples to the new tanks below was pressing, and order must be established. The water in the pools was the main concern, a thing beyond human control, and a matter of constant watchfulness. A remark dropped during the day, of water flowing at night, was not lost on the attentive ear of Joel Wells.

"What did you mean?" he politely inquired of the Running W foreman, while the latter's herd was watering, "of a river only running at night?"

"All over this arid country moisture rises at night and sinks by day," replied the trail boss. "Under drouth, these sandy rivers of the plain, including the Platte and for a thousand miles to the south, only flow at night. It's their protection against the sun's absorption. Mark these pools at sunset and see if they don't rise an inch to-night. Try it and see."

Willow roots were notched on the water-line of each beaver dam. The extreme upper pool was still taking water from a sickly flow, a struggling rivulet, fed by the springs at its head. Doubt was indulged in and freely expressed.

"If the water only holds a week longer," ventured Dell, sleepless in his blankets, "it'll double our holding of cattle."

"It'll hold a month," said Joel, equally sleepless. "We've got to stand by these trail herds--there is no other water short of the Republican. I've figured it all out. When the Beaver ponds are gone, we'll round up the wintered cattle, drift them over to the south fork of the Republican, and get some one to hold them until frost falls. Then we'll ship the cripples up to Hackberry Grove, and that will free the new tanks--water enough for twenty trail herds. We have the horses, and these trail outfits will lend us any help we need. By shifting cattle around, I can see a month's supply. And there may be something in water rising at night. We'll know in the morning."

Sleep blotted out the night. Dawn revealed the fact that the trail foreman knew the secrets of the plain. "That trail boss knew," shouted Joel, rushing into the tent and awakening Dell. "The water rose in every pool. The lower one gained an inch and the upper one gained two. The creek is running freely. The water must be rising out of the ground. Let those Texans bring on their herds. We have oceans of water!"

The cattle came. The first week thirty herds passed the new ranch. It took riding. The dead-line was held, the flotsam cared for, and a hand was ever ready to point a herd or nurse the drag end. Open house was maintained. Every arriving foreman was tendered a horse, and left his benediction on the Beaver.

The ranch proved a haven to man and beast. One of the first foremen to arrive during the second week was Nat Straw. He drove up at sunset, with a chuck-wagon, halted at the tent, and in his usual easy manner inquired, "Where is the matron of this hospital?"

"Here she is," answered Dell, recognizing the man and surmising the situation. "One of your men hurt?"

"Not seriously," answered Straw, looking back into the wagon. "Just a little touch of the dengue. He's been drinking stagnant water, out of cow tracks, for the last few months, and that gets into the bones of the best of us. I'm not feeling very well myself."

Dell lifted the wagon-sheet and peered inside. "Let's get the poor fellow into the tent," urged the boy. "Can he walk, or can you and I carry him?"

"He's the long size Texan, and we'd better try and trail him in," answered Straw, alighting from the wagon. "Where's Dr. Joel Wells?"

"Riding the dead-line. He'll be in shortly. I'll fix a cot, and we'll bring the sick man in at once."

It was simple malaria, known in the Southwest as dengue fever. The unfortunate lad was made comfortable, and on Joel riding in, Straw had skirmished some corn, and was feeding his mules.

"As one of the founders of this hospital," said Straw, after greeting Joel, "this corn has my approval. It is my orders, as one of the trustees, that it be kept in stock hereafter. This team has to go back to the Prairie Dog to-night, and this corn will fortify them for the trip."

The situation was explained. "I only lost half a day," continued Straw, "by bringing the poor fellow over to you. He's one of the best men that ever worked for me, and a month's rest will put him on his feet again. Now, if one of you boys will take the team back to--"

"Certainly," answered Joel. "Anything a director of this hospital wants done--We're running a relief station now--watering the entire drive this year. Where's your outfit camped?"

"A mile above the trail crossing on the Prairie Dog. The wagon's empty. Leave here at two o'clock to-night, and you'll get there in time for breakfast."

"I'm your man. Going to the Prairie Dog at night, in the summer, is a horse that's easy curried."

The next evening Joel brought in Straw's herd. In the mean time the sick man had been cared for, and the passing wayfarer and his cattle made welcome and sped on their way. During the lay-over, Straw had lost his place in the overland march, two herds having passed him and crossed the Beaver.

"I'm corporal here to-day," said Straw to the two foremen, who arrived together in advance. "On this water, I'm the squatter that'll rob you right. You'll count your cattle to me and pay the bill in advance. This cool, shaded water in the Beaver is worth three cents a head, and I'll count you down to a toddling calf and your wagon mules. Your drafts are refused honor at the Beaver banks--nothing but the long green passes currency here. You varmints must show some regrets for taking advantage of a widow woman. I'll make you sorry for passing me."

"How I love to hear old Nat rattle his little song," said one of the foremen, shaking hands with Dell. "Remember the night you slept with me? How's the black cow I gave you last summer?"

Dell fairly clung to the grasped hand. "Pressnell's foreman!" said he, recalling both man and incident. "The cow has a roan calf. Sit down. Will you need a fresh horse to-day? Do you like lettuce?"

"I reckon, Nat," said the other foreman, an hour later, as the two mounted loaned horses, "I reckon your big talk goes up in smoke. You're not the only director in this cattle company. Dell, ransack both our wagons to-day, and see if you can't unearth some dainties for this sick lad. No use looking in Straw's commissary; he never has anything to eat; Injuns won't go near his wagon."

Straw spent a second night with the sick man. On leaving in the morning, he took the feverish hand of the lad and said: "Now, Jack, make yourself right at home. These boys have been tried before, and they're our people. I'm leaving you a saddle and a horse, and when you get on your feet, take your own bearings. You can always count on a job with me, and I'll see that you draw wages until my outfit is relieved. This fever will burn itself out in a week or ten days. I'll keep an eye over you until you are well. S'long, Jack."

The second week fell short only two herds of the previous one. There were fully as many cattle passed, and under the heat of advancing summer the pools suffered a thirsty levy. The resources of the ponds were a constant source of surprise, as an occasional heavy beef caved a foot into an old beaver warren, which poured its contents into the pools. At the end of the first fortnight, after watering fifty-eight herds, nearly half the original quantity of water was still in reserve.

A third week passed. There was a decided falling off in the arrival of herds, only twenty-two crossing the Beaver. The water reserves suffered freely, more from the sun's absorption than from cattle, until the supply became a matter of the most serious concern. The pools would not have averaged a foot in depth, the flow from the springs was a mere trickle, the beaver burrows sounded empty to a horse's footbeat, and there must be some limit to the amount the parched soil would yield.

The brothers found apt counsel in their guest. By the end of the second week, the fever had run its course, and the sick man, Jack Sargent, was up and observant of the situation. True to his calling, he felt for the cattle, and knew the importance of water on the Beaver to the passing drive.

"You must rest these beaver ponds," said Jack, in meeting the emergency. "Every time these pools lower an inch, it gives the sun an advantage. It's absorption that's swallowing up the ponds. You must deepen these pools, which will keep the water cooler. Rest these ponds a few days, or only water late at night. You have water for weeks yet, but don't let the sun rob you. These ponds are living springs compared to some of the water we used south of Red River. Meet the herds on the divide, and pilot the early ones to the tanks below, and the late ones in here. Shifting in your saddle rests a horse, and a little shifting will save your water."

The advice was acted on. While convalescent, Sargent was installed as host on the Beaver, and the brothers took to their saddles. The majority of the herds were met on the Prairie Dog, and after a consultation with the foremen their cattle were started so as to reach the tanks by day or the ranch at evening. The month rounded out with the arrival of eighteen herds, only six of which touched at headquarters, and the fourth week saw a distinct gain in the water supply at the beaver dams. The boys barely touched at home, to change horses, living with the trail wagons, piloting in herds, rich in the reward of relieving the wayfaring, and content with the crumbs that fell to their range.

The drouth of 1886 left a gruesome record in the pastoral history of the West. The southern end of the Texas and Montana cattle trail was marked by the bones of forty thousand cattle that fell, due to the want of water, during the months of travail on that long march. Some of this loss was due to man's inhumanity to the cattle of the fields, in withholding water, but no such charge rested on the owners of the little ranch on the Beaver.

A short month witnessed the beginning of the end of the year's drive. Only such herds as were compelled to, and those that had strength in reserve, dared the plain between the Arkansas and Platte Rivers. The fifth week only six herds arrived, all of which touched at the ranch; half of them had been purchased at Dodge, had neither a cripple nor a stray to bestow, but shared the welcome water and passed on.

One of the purchased herds brought a welcome letter to Joel. It was from Don Lovell, urgently accenting anew his previous invitation to come to Dodge and look over the market.

"After an absence of several weeks," wrote Mr. Lovell, "I have returned to Dodge. From a buyer's standpoint, the market is inviting. The boom prices which prevailed in '84 are cut in half. Any investment in cattle now is perfectly safe.

"I have ordered three of my outfits to return here. They will pass your ranch. Fall in with the first one that comes along. Bring a mount of horses, and report to me on arriving. Fully half this year's drive is here, unsold. Be sure and come."

"Are you going?" inquired Dell on reading the letter.

"I am," answered Joel with emphasis.

"That's the talk," said Sargent. "Whenever cattle get so cheap that no other man will look a cow in the face, that's the time to buy her. Folks are like sheep; the Bible says so; they all want to buy or all want to sell. I only know Mr. Lovell from what you boys have told me; but by ordering three outfits to return to Dodge, I can see that he's going to take advantage of that market and buy about ten thousand cattle. You've got the range. Buy this summer. I'll stay with Dell until you return. Buy a whole herd of steers, and I'll help you hold them this winter."

The scene shifted. Instead of looking to the south for a dust cloud, the slopes of the north were scanned for an approaching cavalcade. The last week admitted of taking an account of the cattle dropped at the new ranch. From the conserves of its owners, one hundred and four herds had watered, over three hundred thousand cattle, the sweepings of which amounted to a few over eleven hundred head, fully fifty of which, exhausted beyond recovery, died after reaching their new range.

By the end of July, only an occasional herd was arriving. August was ushered in with the appearance of Bob Quirk, one of the division foremen, on the upper march. He arrived early in the morning, in advance of his outfit barely an hour, and inquired for Joel. Dell answered for the brothers, the older one and Sargent being above at Hackberry Grove.

"I have orders to bring him to Dodge," said Quirk, dismounting. "Make haste and bring in the remuda. We'll cut him out a mount of six horses and throw them in with mine. Joel can follow on the seventh. My outfit will barely touch here in passing. We're due to receive cattle in Dodge on the 5th, and time is precious. Joel can overtake us before night. Make haste."

CHAPTER XVI.
A PROTECTED CREDIT

The trail outfit swept past the ranch, leaving Dell on nettles. The importance of the message was urgent, and saddling up a horse, he started up the Beaver in search of Joel and Sargent. They were met returning, near the dead-line, and after listening to the breathless report, the trio gave free rein to their horses on the homeward ride.

"I'll use old Rowdy for my seventh horse," said Joel, swinging out of the saddle at the home corral. "Bring him in and give him a feed of corn. It may be late when I overtake the outfit. Mr. Quince says that that old horse has cow-sense to burn; that he can scent a camp at night, or trail a remuda like a hound."

An hour later Joel cantered up to the tent. "This may be a wild-goose chase," said he, "but I'm off. If my hopes fall dead, I can make a hand coming back. Sargent, if I do buy any cattle, your name goes on the pay-roll from to-day. I'll leave you in charge of the ranch, anyhow. There isn't much to do except to ride the dead-line twice a day. The wintered cattle are located; and the cripples below--the water and their condition will hold them. Keep open house, and amuse yourselves the best you can. That's about all I can think of just now."

Joel rode away in serious meditation. Although aged beyond his years, he was only seventeen. That he could ride into Dodge City, the far-famed trail-town of the West, and without visible resources buy cattle, was a fit subject for musing. There the drovers from Texas and the ranchmen from the north and west met and bartered for herds--where the drive of the year amounted to millions in value. Still the boy carried a pressing invitation from a leading drover to come, and neither slacking rein nor looking back, he was soon swallowed up in the heat-waves over the plain.

Sargent and Dell sought the shelter of the awning. "Well," said the latter, "that trip's a wild-goose chase. How he expects to buy cattle without money gets me."

"It may be easier than it seems," answered Sargent. "You secured a start in cattle last summer without money. Suppose you save a thousand head out of the cripples this year, what have they cost you?"

"That's different," protested Dell. "Dodge City is a market where buyers and sellers meet."

"True enough. And behind that are unseen conditions. The boom of two years ago in land and live stock bankrupted many people in Texas. Cattle companies were organized on the very summit of that craze. Then came the slump. Last year cattle had fallen in price nearly forty per cent. This year there is a further falling. I'm giving you Texas conditions. Half the herds at Dodge to-day are being handled by the receivers of cattle companies or by trustees for banks. That accounts for the big drive. Then this drouth came on, and the offerings at Dodge are unfit for any purpose, except to restock ranches. And those northern ranchmen know it. They'll buy the cattle at their own price and pay for them when they get good and ready."

Dell was contending for his view. "Do you claim that a northern cowman can buy cattle from a Texas drover without money?"

"Certainly. When one sheep jumps off the cliff and breaks his neck, all the rest jump off and break their necks. When money is pouring into cattle, as it was two years ago, range cattle were as good as gold. Now, when all that investment is trying to withdraw from cattle, they become a drag on the market. The Simple Simons ain't all dead yet. Joel will buy cattle."

"He may, but I don't see how."

"Buy them just as any other wide-awake cowman. You brothers are known in Dodge. This water that you have given the drovers, during the drouth, has made you friends. Mr. Lovell's word, in your behalf, is as good as money in the bank. Joel will come back with cattle. My only fear is, he won't strain his credit."

"Credit! Who would credit us?"

"Why not? There are not so many drovers at Dodge who had your showing at the same age. They have fought their way up and know who to credit. Your range and ability to hold cattle are your best assets. We must shape up the ranch, because Joel will come in with cattle."

"You're the foreman," said Dell assentingly. "And what's more, if Joel comes home with cattle, I'll hit the ground with my hat and shout as loud as any of you."

"That's the talk. I'm playing Joel to come back winner. Let's saddle up horses, and ride through the cripples this afternoon. I want to get the lay of the range, and the water, and a line on the cattle."

Joel overtook Bob Quirk midway between the Prairie Dog and the railroad. The outfit was drifting south at the rate of forty miles a day, traveling early and late to avoid the heat. On sighting the lone horseman in the rear, signals were exchanged, and the foreman halted until Joel overtook the travelers.

"This is the back track," said Quirk, "and we're expected to crowd three days into one. I don't know what the old man wants with you, but I had a wire to pick you up."

"Mr. Lovell has been urging me to stock our range--to buy more cattle," admitted Joel.

"That's what I thought. He's buying right and left. We're on our way now to receive cattle. That's it; the old man has a bunch of cattle in sight for you."

"Possibly. But what's worrying me is, how am I to buy them--if it takes any money!" dejectedly admitted the husky boy.

"Is that fretting you?" lightly inquired Quirk. "Let the old man do the worrying--that's his long suit. You can rest easy that he has everything all figured out. It might keep you and I guessing, but it's as clear as mud to that old man. We'll make Dodge in four days."

The ravages of the drouth were disheartening. A few hours after sunrise, a white haze settled over the dull, dead plain, the heat-waves rolled up to the cavalcade like a burning prairie, sweat and dust crusted over the horses under saddle, without variation of pace or course. Only three herds were met, feeling their way through the mirages, or loitering along the waters. Traveling by night was preferable, and timing the route into camps and marches, the cottonwood on the Arkansas River was sighted in advance of the schedule.

The outfit halted on a creek north of town. Cattle under herd had been sighted by the thousands, and before the camp was made snug, a conveyance drove up and Forrest and Don Lovell alighted.

"Well, Bob, you're a little ahead of time," said the latter, amid general greetings, "but I'm glad of it. I've closed trades on enough cattle to make up a herd, and the sellers are hurrying me to receive them. Pick up a full outfit of men to-night, and we'll receive to-morrow afternoon. Quince took the train at Cheyenne, but his outfit ought to reach here in a day or so. I've laid my tape on this market, and have all the cattle in sight that I want. Several deals are pending, awaiting the arrival of this boy. Come to town to-night. I'll take Joel under my wing right now."

Three horses were caught, Joel riding one and leading two, and the vehicle started. It was still early in the afternoon, and following down the creek, within an hour the party reached a trail wagon encamped. A number of men were about, including a foreman; and at the request of Mr. Lovell to look over their cattle and horses again the camp took on an air of activity. A small remuda was corralled within ropes, running from choice to common horses, all of which were looked over carefully by the trio, including the wagon team. A number of horses were under saddle, and led by the foreman, a quartette of men started in advance to bunch the herd.

Leaving Forrest at the camp, Mr. Lovell and Joel took the rig and leisurely followed the departing horsemen. "This is one of the best herds on the market," said the old drover to the boy, "and I've kept the deal pending, to see if you and I couldn't buy it together. It runs full thirty-five hundred cattle, twelve hundred threes and the remainder twos. I always buy straight two-year-olds for my beef ranch, because I double-winter all my steer cattle--it takes two winters in the north to finish these Texas steers right. Now, if you can handle the threes, the remnant of twos, and the saddle stock, we'll buy the herd, lock, stock, and barrel. The threes will all ship out as four-year-old beeves next fall, and you can double-winter the younger cattle. I can use two thousand of the two-year-olds, and if you care for the others, after we look them over, leave me to close the trade."

"Mr. Lovell, it has never been clear to me how I am to buy cattle without money," earnestly said Joel.

"Leave that to me--I have that all figured out. If we buy this herd together, you can ship out two thousand beef cattle next fall, and a ranch that has that many beeves to market a year hence, can buy, with or without money, any herd at Dodge to-day. If you like the cattle and want them, leave it all to me."

"But so many horses--We have forty horses already," protested Joel.

"A wide-awake cowman, in this upper country, always buys these southern horses a year in advance of when he needs them. Next year you'll be running a shipping outfit, mounting a dozen men, sending others on fall round-ups, and if you buy your horses now, you'll have them in the pink of condition then. It's a small remuda, a few under sixty horses, as fifty head were detailed out here to strengthen remudas that had to go to the Yellowstone. This foreman will tell you that he topped out twenty-five of the choice horses before the other trail bosses were allowed to pick. As the remuda stands, its make-up is tops and tailings. A year hence one will be as good as the other. You'll need the horses, and by buying down to the blanket, turning the owner foot-loose and free, it will help me to close the trade, in our mutual interest."

The cattle were some two miles distant, under close herd, and by quietly edging them in onto a few hundred acres, they could be easily looked over from the conveyance. On the arrival of the prospective buyers, the foreman had the cattle sufficiently compact, and the old man and the boy drove back and forth through the herd for fully an hour. They were thrifty, western Texas steers, had missed the drouth by coming into the trail at Camp Supply, and were all that could be desired in range cattle. The two agreed on the quality of the herd, and on driving out from among the cattle, the foreman was signaled up.

"One of my outfits arrived from the Platte this afternoon," said Mr. Lovell, "and we'll receive to-morrow. That leaves me free to pick up another herd. If Dud would try his best, he would come very near selling me these cattle. I've got a buyer in sight for the threes and remnant of twos, and if you price the horses right, we might leave you afoot. If you see Dudley before I do, tell him I looked over his cattle again."

"I'll see him to-night," said the foreman, calling after the vehicle.

Forrest was picked up, and they returned to town. The fame of wicked Dodge never interfered with the transaction of business, its iniquity catering largely to the rabble.

"I'll take Joel with me," said the drover to Forrest, "and you look after the horses and hang around the hotel. Dud Stoddard is almost sure to look me up, and if you meet him, admit that we looked over his cattle again. I want him to hound me into buying that herd."

Joel's taciturn manner stood him in good stead. He was alert to all that was passing and, except with Mr. Lovell, was reticent in the extreme. The two strolled about the streets during the evening hours, and on returning to the hotel rather late, Dudley Stoddard was awaiting the old drover. There was no prelude to the matter at issue, and after arranging with other sellers to receive the following day, Mr. Lovell led the way to his room.

"This is one of the Wells Brothers," said the old cowman, presenting Joel; "one of the boys who watered the drive on the Beaver this summer. I was up on his ranch about a month ago, and gave him a good scolding for not stocking his range somewhere near its carrying capacity. He's the buyer I had in view for your three-year-olds. You offered me the herd, on time, and at satisfactory prices. I can use two thousand of the twos, and Wells Brothers will take the remainder, and we'll turn you afoot. Say so, and your herd is sold."

"Well," said Mr. Stoddard, somewhat embarrassed, "I don't happen to know the Wells Brothers--and I usually know men when I extend them a credit. This boy--Well, I'm not in the habit of dealing with boys."

"You and I were boys once and had to make our start," testily replied Mr. Lovell, pacing the room. "The Wells Brothers are making the fight that you and I were making twenty years ago. In our early struggles, had some one stood behind us, merely stood behind us, it might have been different with us to-day. And now when I don't need no help--Dud, it don't cost much to help others. These boys have proven themselves white, to yours and to my men and to yours and to my cattle. Is there nothing we can do?"

Mr. Stoddard turned to the old drover. "I'll renew my last offer to you. Take the herd and sell these boys the older cattle and remnants. You know the brothers--you know their resources."

"No!" came the answer like a rifle-shot.

"Then, will you stand sponsor--will you go their security?"

"No! These boys can't send home for money nor can't borrow any. Their only asset is their ability to hold and mature cattle. Last winter, the most severe one in the history of the West, they lost two per cent of their holdings. Neither you nor I can make as good a showing on any of our ranges. Dud, what I'm trying to do is to throw on this boy's shoulders the *responsibility* of *paying* for *any cattle he buys*. At his age it would be wrong to rob him of that important lesson. Let's you and I stand behind him, and let's see to it that he makes the right effort to protect his credit."

"That's different," admitted Mr. Stoddard. "Don, if you'll suggest the means to that end, I'll try and meet you halfway."

Mr. Lovell took a seat at the table and picked up a blank sheet of paper. "As mutual friends," said he, "let me draw up, from seller to buyer, an iron-clad bill of sale. Its first clause will be a vendor's lien for the cost of the cattle, horses, etc. Its second will be the appointment of a commission house, who will act as agent, hold this contract, and receive the beeves when ready for shipment to market. Its third clause will be your right, as creditor in a sale of chattel, to place a man of your own selection on Wells Brothers' ranch, under their pay and subject to their orders. As your representative, the privilege is granted of making a daily, weekly, or monthly report to you of the condition of the cattle and the general outlook of the buyers to meet this, their covenant with the seller, before November 1, 1887.

"I wouldn't enter into such a contract with you," continued Mr. Lovell, throwing down the sheet of paper, "but I want this boy to learn the value of a well-protected credit. At his time of life, it's an asset. I'll pay for my half when it's convenient, but I want him to meet his first obligation on or before the day of maturity. I can speak for the boy's willingness to make such a contract. What do you say?"

"Delivery here or elsewhere?" inquired Mr. Stoddard.

"My half here, within three days, the remainder on the Beaver, a seven days' drive. It won't cost you a cent more to send your outfit home from Grinnell than from Dodge. Ten days will end all your trouble. What do you say?"

"Don, let me talk the matter over with you privately," said Mr. Stoddard, arising. "The boy will excuse us. We'll give him a square deal."

The two old men left the room. Forrest arose from a couch and threw his arms around Joel. "It's a sale!" he whispered. "The cattle's yours! That old man of mine will ride Dud Stoddard all around the big corral and spur him in the flank at every jump, unless he comes to those terms. An iron-clad bill of sale is its own surety. You'll need the man, anyhow. I want to give the long yell."

Mr. Lovell returned after midnight, and alone. Forrest and Joel arose to meet him, inquiry and concern in every look and action.

"Take Joel and get out of here," said the old drover, whose twinkling eyes could not conceal the gloating within. "I've got to draw up that bill of sale. Just as if those steers wouldn't pay for themselves next fall. Get to bed, you rascals!"

"Would there be any harm if I went down to the bank of the river and gave the long yell?" inquired Forrest, as he halted in the doorway.

"Get to bed," urged the old drover. "I'll want you in the morning. We'll close a trade, the first thing, on fifteen hundred of those Womack twos. That'll give you a herd, and you can keep an eye over Joel's cattle until the Beaver's reached."

During the few days which followed, Joel Wells was thrown in contact with the many features of a range cattle market. In all the migrations of mankind, strictly cattle towns like Dodge City and Ogalalla are unknown. They were the product of all pastoral ages, reaching a climax on American soil, and not of record in any other country or time. Joel let little escape him. Here men bought and sold by the thousand head, in his day and generation, and he was a part of that epoch.

The necessary number of cattle to complete a herd for Forrest were purchased without leaving town. The afternoon was spent in receiving a herd, in which the veteran drover took a hand, assisted by two competent foremen. Every feature in the cattle, the why and wherefore, was pointed out by the trio, to the eager, earnest boy, so that the lesson sunk into Joel's every fibre. The beauty of the first herd received was in the uniform average of each animal, when ages, class, and build governed selection.

Forrest's outfit arrived that evening, and without even a day's rest arrangements were made to receive the two contingents the next morning. When it came to receive the Stoddard herd, the deftness with which the two outfits classified the cattle was only short of marvelous. The threes were cut out, and each age counted. The over-plus of the younger cattle were cut back, and the contingents were tendered on delivery. The papers were ready, executed on the ground, and the herds started, the smaller in the lead.

The drive to the Beaver was without incident. Forrest spent most of his time with the little herd, which used only eight men, counting Joel, who stood guard at night and made a hand. The herd numbered a few over fifteen hundred cattle, the remuda fifty-six horses, a team and wagon, the total contract price of which was a trifle under twenty-five thousand dollars. It looked like a serious obligation for two boys to assume, but practical men had sanctioned it, and it remained for the ability of Wells Brothers to meet it.

On nearing the Beaver, the lead herd under Bob Quirk took the new trail, which crossed at the ranch. On their leaving the valley, a remark was dropped, unnoticed by Dell, but significant to Jack Sargent. It resulted in the two riding out on the trail, only to meet the purchased cattle, Joel on one point and Forrest on the other, directing the herds to the tanks below. The action bespoke its intent, and on meeting Forrest, the latter jerked his thumb over his shoulder, remarking, "Drop back and pilot the wagon and remuda into the ranch. We're taking this passel of cattle into the new tanks, and will scatter them up and down the creek. Lovell's cattle? No. Old man Joel Wells bought these to stock his ranch. See how chesty it makes him--he won't even look this way. You boys may have to sit up with him a few nights at first, but he'll get over that. Pilot in the remuda. You two are slated to take this outfit to the railroad to-night. Trail along, my beauties; Wells Brothers are shaking out a right smart bit of sail these days."

CHAPTER XVII.
"THE WAGON"

The little ranch had assumed a contract and must answer at the appointed time. If the brothers could meet their first commercial obligation, it would establish their standing, and to that end every energy must be directed. They were extremely fortunate in the advice and help of two young men bred to the occupation, and whose every interest lay in making a success of the ranch.

The trail outfit returned to the railroad that night. Everything was abandoned but their saddles--*burning the wagon*--while Joe Manly, one of their number, remained behind. Manly was not even the foreman, and on taking his departure the trail boss, in the presence of all, said to his man, "Now, Joe, turn yourself over to this ranch and make a useful hand. Drop old man Dudley a line whenever you have a chance. It's quite a little ride to the station, and we'll understand that no news is good news. And once you see that these cattle are going to winter safely, better raise the long yell and come home. You can drift back in the fall--during the beef-shipping season. I may write you when next summer's plans begin to unfold."

Accompanied by Dell and Sargent, and singing the home songs of the South, the outfit faded away into the night. Forrest's herd had watered during the evening, and moved out to a safe camp, leaving its foreman on the Beaver. He and Manly discussed the situation, paving the way in detail, up to the manner of holding the cattle during the coming winter. With numbers exceeding three thousand, close herd and corralling at night was impossible, and the riding of lines, with an extra camp, admitting of the widest freedom, was decided on as the most feasible method. The new camp must be located well above Hackberry Grove, and to provision it for man and horse was one of the many details outlined in meeting the coming winter. Joel was an attentive listener, and having held cattle by one system, he fully understood the necessity of adopting some other manner of restraint. In locating cattle, where there was danger of drifting from any cause, the method of riding lines was simple and easily understood--to patrol the line liable to assault from drifting cattle.

Forrest was elated over the outlook. On leaving the next morning, he turned his horse and rode back to the tent. "This may be the last time I'll come this way," said he to Joel, "as there is talk of the trail moving west. On account of fever, this State threatens to quarantine against Texas cattle. If it does, the trail will have to move over into Colorado or hunt a new route through unorganized counties on the western line of Kansas. In event of quarantine being enforced, it means a bigger range for Wells Brothers. Of course, this is only your second year in cattle, just getting a firm grip on the business, but I can see a big future for you boys. As cowmen, you're just in swaddling clothes yet, toddling around on your first legs, but the outlook is rosy. Hold these cattle this winter, protect your credit next fall, and it doesn't matter if I never come back. A year hence you'll have a bank account, be living on the sunny side of the creek, and as long as you stick to cows, through thick and thin, nothing can unhorse you."

The trail foreman rode away to overtake his herd, and Joel and Manly busied themselves in locating the new cattle. Dell and Sargent accompanied the last Lovell herd into the ranch that evening, and it proved to be the rear guard of trail cattle for that summer.

The ranch was set in order for the present. The dead-line was narrowed to a mile, which admitted of fully half the through cattle watering at the beaver ponds around headquarters. The new remuda, including all horses acquired that summer, to the number of eighty head, was moved up to Hackberry Grove and freed for the year. The wintered horses furnished ample saddle mounts for the present, there being little to do, as the water held the new cattle and no herding was required. The heat of summer was over, the water held in tanks and beaver dams, and the ranch settled down in pastoral security.

Under the new outline for the winter, an increased amount of forage must be provided, as in riding lines two grain-fed horses to the man was the lowest limit in mounting all line-riders. Machinery was available on the railroad, and taking a team, Joel returned with a new mowing machine, and the matter of providing abundant forage was easily met. Sufficient hay, from a few bends of the creek, in dead-line territory, supplied the home ranch, and a week's encampment above Hackberry Grove saw the site of the new line-camp equipped with winter forage.

While engaged on the latter task, a new feature was introduced on Wells Brothers' ranch. A movable commissary is a distinct aid to any pastoral occupation, and hence *the wagon* becomes a cowman's home and castle. From it he dispenses a rough hospitality, welcomes the wayfarer, and exchanges the chronicle of the range. The wagon, which had been acquired with the new herd and used on the above occasion, was well equipped with canvas cover, water barrels, and a convenient chuck-box at the rear. The latter was fitted with drawers and compartments as conveniently as a kitchen. When open, the lid of the box afforded a table; when closed, it protected the contents from the outer elements. The wagon thus becomes home to nomadic man and animal, the one equal with the other. Saddle horses, when frightened at night, will rush to the safety of a camp-fire and the protection of their masters, and therefore a closer bond exists between the men of the open and their mounts than under more refined surroundings.

Early in September a heavy rain fell in the west, extending down the Beaver, flushing the creek and providing an abundance of running water. It was followed by early frosts, lifting the dead-line and ushering in Indian summer. With forage secure, attention was turned to the cattle. The purchase of a mowing machine had exhausted the funds derived from the sale of peltry, and a shipment of cattle was decided on to provide the munitions for the coming winter. The wagon was accordingly provisioned for a week, the blankets stored in the commissary, and the quartette moved out to round up the wintered cattle. They had not been handled since the spring drift of March before, and when thrown into a compact herd, they presented a different appearance from the spiritless cattle of six months previous. A hundred calves, timid as fawns, shied from the horsemen, their mothers lowed in comforting concern, the beeves waddled about from carrying their own flesh, while the patriarchs of the herd bellowed in sullen defiance. Fifty of the heaviest beeves were cut out from the ---- Y brand, flesh governing the selection, and the first shipment of cattle left the Beaver for eastern markets.

Four days were required to graze the heavy cattle down to the railroad. Dell drove the wagon, Sargent was intrusted with the remuda, the two others grazing the beeves, while each took his turn in standing guard at night. Water was plentiful, cars were in waiting, and on reaching the railroad, the cattle were corralled in the shipping pens.

Joel and Manly accompanied the shipment to Kansas City. The beeves were consigned to the firm mentioned in the bill of sale as factor in marketing and settlement of the herd which had recently passed from the possession of Mr. Stoddard to that of Wells Brothers. The two cars of cattle found a ready sale, the weights revealing a surprise, attracting the attention of packers and salesmen to the quality of beef from the Beaver valley.

"Give me the cattle from the short-grass country," said a salesman to a packer, as Wells Brothers' beeves were crossing the weighing scale. "You and I needn't worry about the question of range--the buffalo knew. Catch the weights of these cattle and compare it with range beef from the sedge-grass and mountain country. Tallow tells its own story--the buffalo knew the best range."

An acquaintance with the commission house was established on a mutual basis. The senior member of the firm, a practical old man, detained Joel and Manly in his private office for an hour.

"This market is alert to every new section having cattle to ship," said the old man to Joel, studying a sales statement. "The Solomon River country sent in some cattle last fall, but yours is the first shipment from the Beaver. Our salesman reports your consignment the fattest range beeves on to-day's market. And these weights confirm the statement. I don't understand it. What kind of a country have you out there?"

Joel gave Manly an appealing look. "It's the plains," answered the latter. "It's an old buffalo range. You can see their skulls by the thousand. It's a big country; it just swells, and dips, and rolls away."

It was the basis of a range which interested the senior member. "The grasses, the grasses?" he repeated. "What are your native grasses?"

"Oh, just plain, every-day buffalo grass," answered Manly. "Of course, here and there, in the bends of the Beaver, there's a little blue-stem, enough for winter forage for the saddle stock. The cattle won't touch it."

The last of many subjects discussed was the existing contract, of which the commission firm was the intermediary factor. The details were gone over carefully, the outlook for next year's shipments reviewed, and on taking their leave, the old man said to his guests:--

"Well, I'm pleased over the outlook. The firm have had letters from both Mr. Lovell and Mr. Stoddard, and now that I've gone over the situation, with the boys in the saddle, everything is clear and satisfactory. Next year's shipments will take care of the contract. Keep in touch with us, and we'll advise you from time to time. Ship your cattle in finished condition, and they'll make a market for themselves. We'll expect you early next summer."

"Our first shipment will be two hundred double-wintered cattle," modestly admitted Joel.

"They ought to be ready a full month in advance of your single-wintered beeves," said the old man, from his practical knowledge in maturing beef. "Ship them early. The bookkeeper has your account all ready."

Joel and Manly were detained at the business office only a moment. The beeves had netted thirty-five dollars a head, and except for current expenses, the funds were left on deposit with the commission house, as there were no banks near home; the account was subject to draft, and accepting a small advance in currency, the boys departed. A brief hour's shopping was indulged in, the principal purchases being two long-range rifles, cartridges and poison in abundance, when they hastened to the depot and caught a west-bound train. Horses had been left at Grinnell, and at evening the next day the two rode into headquarters on the Beaver.

Beyond question there are tides in the affairs of men. With the first shipment of cattle from the little ranch, poverty fled and an air of independence indicated the turn in the swing of the pendulum. Practical men, in every avenue of the occupation, had lent their indorsement to the venture of the brothers, the mettle of the pasture had been tested in the markets, and the future, with reasonable vigilance, rested on sure foundations.

The turn of the tide was noticeable at once. "I really think Uncle Dud would let me come home," said Manly to the others, at supper. "There's no occasion for my staying here this winter. Besides, I'm a tender plant; I'm as afraid of cold as a darky is of thunder. Wouldn't I like to get a letter from Uncle Dud saying, 'Come home, my little white chicken, come home!'"

"You can go in the spring," said Joel. "We're going to use four line-riders this winter, and there's every reason why you'll make a trusty one!"

"That's one of the owners talking," observed Sargent; "now listen to the foreman's orders: The next thing is to brand every hoof up to date. Then, at the upper line-camp, comes the building of a new dug-out and stabling for four horses. And lastly, freight in plenty of corn. After that, if we fail to hold the cattle, it's our own fault. No excuse will pass muster. Hold these cattle? It's a dead immortal cinch! Joseph dear, make yourself a useful guest for the winter."

A hopeful spirit lightened every task. The calves and their mothers were brought down to the home corral and branded in a single day. The Stoddard cattle, the title being conditional, were exempt, the Lazy H ranch brand fully protecting mutual interests. Only cripple, fagged, and stray cattle were branded, the latter numbering less than a hundred head, and were run into the Hospital brand, while the remainder bore the--Y of the ranch. The work was completed within a week, Dell making a hand which proved his nerve, either in the saddle or branding pen.

The first week in October was devoted to building the new dug-out and stable. The wagon was provisioned, every implement and tool on the ranch, from a hammer to a plough, was taken along, as well as the remuda, and the quartette sallied forth to the task as if it were a frolic. The site had been decided on during the haying, and on reaching the scene, the tent was set up, and the building of a shelter for man and horse was begun.

The dug-out of the West is built for comfort,--half cellar and the remainder sod walls. A southern slope was selected; an abrupt break or low bank was taken advantage of, admitting of four-foot cellar walls on three sides, the open end inclosed with massive sod walls and containing the door. The sod was broken by a team and plough, cut into lengths like brick, and the outside walls raised to the desired height. For roofing, a heavy ridge-pole was cut the length of the room, resting on stout upright posts. Lighter poles were split and laid compactly, like rafters, sheeted with hay, and covered with loose dirt to the depth of a foot. The floor was earthen; a half window east and west, supplemented by a door in the south, admitted light, making a cosy, comfortable shelter. A roomy stable was built on the same principle and from the same material.

The work was completed quickly, fuel for the winter gathered, when the quartette started homeward. "It looks like the halfway house at Land's End," said Manly, turning for a last look at the new improvements. "What are you going to call the new tepee?"

"Going to call it The Wagon," answered Sargent, he and Dell having accepted the new line-camp as their winter quarters, "and let the latch-string hang on the outside. Whenever you can, you must bring your knitting and come over."

CHAPTER XVIII.
AN OPEN WINTER

An ideal Indian summer was enjoyed. Between the early and late fall frosts, the range matured into perfect winter pasturage. Light rains in September freshened the buffalo grass until it greened on the sunny slopes, cured into hay as the fall advanced, thus assuring abundant forage to the cattle.

Manly was the only one of the quartette not inured to a northern climate. A winter in Montana had made Sargent proof against any cold, while the brothers were native to that latitude if not to the plains. After building the line-camp and long before occupying it, the quartette paired off, Sargent and Dell claiming the new dug-out, while the other two were perfectly content with the old shack at headquarters. A healthy spirit of rivalry sprang up, extending from a division of the horses down to a fair assignment of the blankets.

Preparations for and a constant reference to the coming winter aroused a dread in Manly. "You remind me of our darky cook," said Sargent, "up on the Yellowstone a few years ago. Half the trail outfit were detailed until frost, to avoid fever and to locate the cattle, and of course the cook had to stay. A squall of snow caught us in camp, and that poor darky just pined away. 'Boss,' he used to say to the foreman, shivering over the fire, 'ah's got to go home. Ah's subjec' to de rheumatics. Mah fambly's a-gwine to be pow'ful uneasy 'bout me. Dis-a-yere country am no place fo' a po' ol' niggah.'"

Two teams were employed in freighting in the corn, four round trips being required, Joel and Manly assuming the work. Supplies for the winter were brought in at the same time, among the first of which were four sacks of salt; and the curing of two barrels of corned beef fell a pleasant task to Dell and his partner. There was nothing new in pickling the meat, and with the exception of felling the beeves, the incident passed as part of the day's work. Dell claimed the privilege of making the shots, which Sargent granted, but exercised sufficient caution to corral the beeves. Both fell in their tracks, and the novice gained confidence in his skill in the use of a rifle.

The first of December was agreed on to begin the riding of lines. That date found all the new cattle drifted above headquarters, and as it was some ten miles to the upper line-camp, an extremely liberal range was allowed the herd. Eight of the best wintered horses were stabled, and at first the line was maintained on the south bank of the Beaver. An outer line was agreed upon, five miles to the south; but until the season forced the cattle to the shelter of the valley, the inner one was kept under patrol. The outer was a purely imaginary line, extending in an immense half-circle, from headquarters to the new line-camp above. It followed the highest ground, and marked the utmost limit on the winter range on the south. Any sign or trace of cattle crossing it, drifting before a storm or grazing at leisure, must be turned back or trailed down.

The first and second weeks passed, the weather continuing fine. Many of the cattle ranged two and three miles north of the creek, not even coming in to water oftener than every other day. Several times the horsemen circled to the north; but as ranging wide was an advantage, the cattle were never disturbed. A light fall of soft snow even failed to bring the cattle into the valley.

Christmas week was ushered in with a display of animal instinct. The through and wintered cattle had mixed and mingled, the latter fat and furred, forging to the front in ranging northward, and instinctively leading their brethren to shelter in advance of the first storm. Between the morning and evening patrol of a perfect day, the herd, of its own accord, drifted into the valley, the leaders rioting in a wild frolic. Their appearance hastened the patrol of the inner line by an hour, every nook and shelter, including the old corral, being filled with frolicsome cattle. The calves were engaging each other in mimic fights, while the older cattle were scarring every exposed bank, or matting their foreheads in clay and soft dirt.

"What does it mean?" inquired Joel, hailing Sargent, when the line-riders met.

"It means that we'll ride the outside line in the morning," came the reply. "There's a storm coming within twelve hours. At least, the herd say so."

"What can we do?"

"Leave that to the cattle. They'll not quit the valley unless driven out by a storm. The instinct that teaches them of the coming storm also teaches them how to meet it. They'll bed in the blue-stem to-night, or hunt a cosy nook under some cut-bank."

A meeting point on the outer line, for the next morning, was agreed upon, when the horsemen separated for the evening. "Get out early, and keep your eyes open for any trace of cattle crossing the line," Sargent called back, as he reined homeward. "Dell and I will leave The Wagon at daybreak."

The storm struck between midnight and morning. Dawn revealed an angry horizon, accompanied by a raw, blue-cold, cutting wind from the north. On leaving their quarters, both patrols caught the storm on an angle, edging in to follow the circle, their mounts snorting defiance and warming to the work in resisting the bitter morning. The light advanced slowly, a sifting frost filled the air, obscuring the valley, and not until the slope to the south was reached was the situation known.

No cattle were in sight or adrift. Within an hour after leaving the line-camp, the experienced eye of Sargent detected a scattering trace where an unknown number of cattle had crossed the line. Both he and Dell dismounted, and after studying the trail, its approach and departure, the range-bred man was able to give a perfect summary of the situation.

"There's between fifty and a hundred head in this drift," remarked Sargent, as the two remounted. "They're through cattle; the storm must have caught them on the divide, north of the Beaver. They struck the creek in the flats and were driven out of the valley. The trail's not over two hours old. Ride the line until you meet the other boys, and I'll trail down these cattle. The sand dunes ought to catch them."

Dell and Sargent separated. Five miles to the eastward Joel was met. Manly was reported at the rear, the two having intercepted a contingent of cattle approaching the line, and was then drifting the stragglers back to the valley. On Dell's report, the brothers turned to the assistance of Sargent, retracing the western line, and finally bearing off for the sand hills. Several times the sun threatened to break through, lighting the valley, but without revealing any stir among the cattle in the shelter of the creek. In the short time since leaving their stables, the horses under saddle had whitened from the action of the frost on their sweaty coats, unheeded by their riders. There was no checking of mounts until the range of dunes was reached, when from the summit of a sand hill the stragglers were located in care of Sargent, and on the homeward drift. The cattle were so benumbed and bewildered from the cold that they had marched through the shelter of the dunes, and were overtaken adrift on the wind-swept plain.

The contingent numbered sixty-odd cattle, and with the help of the brothers were easily handled. Before recrossing the line, the sun burst forth, and on reaching the slope, the trio halted in parting. "A few hours of this sun," said Sargent, "and we've got the upper hand of this storm. The wind or sun must yield. If the wind lulls, we'll ride the inner line to-night and bed every hoof in the shelter of the creek. Pick up Manly, and we'll ride the valley line about the middle of the afternoon."

Joel turned homeward, scouting that portion of the line under patrol from headquarters. The drifting contingent was intrusted to Dell, leaving Sargent to retrace their division of the line, and before noon all had reached their quarters. From twenty to thirty miles had been covered that morning, in riding the line and recovering the lost, and at the agreed time, the relay horses were under saddle for the afternoon task. The sun had held sway, the wind had fallen, and as they followed up the valley, they encountered the cattle in large bunches, grazing to every quarter of the compass. They were not molested on the outward ride, but on the return trip, near evening, they were all turned back to the sheltering nooks and coves which the bends of the Beaver afforded. A crimpy night followed, but an early patrol in the morning found the cattle snug in the dry, rank grasses which grew in the first bottoms of the creek.

The first storm had been weathered. The third day, of their own accord, the cattle left the valley and grazed out on the northern divide. The line-riders relaxed their vigil, and in preparation for observing the Natal day, each camp put forth its best hunter to secure a venison. The absence of snow, during the storm, had held the antelope tributary to the Beaver, and locating game was an easy matter. To provide the roast, the spirit of rivalry was accented anew, and each camp fervently hoped for its own success.

A venison hung at headquarters before noon, Manly making a running shot at the leader of a band, which was surprised out of a morning siesta near the old trail crossing. If a quarry could only be found in the sand hills, a natural shelter for antelope, Sargent had flattered Dell into believing that his aim was equal to the occasion. The broken nature of the dune country admitted of stealthy approach, and its nearness to the upper camp recommended it as an inviting hunting ground. The disappointment of the first effort, due to moderated weather, was in finding the quarry far afield. A dozen bands were sighted from the protection of the sand hills, a mile out on the flat plain, but without shelter to screen a hunter. Sargent was equal to the occasion, and selecting a quarry, the two horses were unsaddled, the bridle reins lengthened by adding ropes, and crouching low, their mounts afforded the necessary screen as they grazed or were driven forward. By tacking right and left in a zigzag course they gained the wind, and a stealthy approach on the band was begun. The stabled horses grazed ravenously, sometimes together, then apart, affording a perfect screen for stalking.

After a seeming age to Dell, the required rifle range was reached, when the cronies flattened themselves in the short grass and allowed the horses to graze to their rope's end. Sargent indicated a sentinel buck, presenting the best shot; and using his elbow for a rest, the rifle was laid in the hollow of Dell's upraised hand and drawn firmly to his shoulder, and a prompt report followed. The shot went wild, throwing up a flash of dust before the band, which instantly whirled. The horses merely threw up their heads in surprise, attracting the startled quarry, which ran up within fifty yards of the repeating rifle. In the excitement of the moment instantly following the first shot, Dell had arisen to his knee, unmindful of the necessity of throwing another cartridge into the rifle barrel. "Shoot! Shoot!" whispered Sargent, as the band excitedly halted within pistol range. Dell fingered the trigger in vain. "Throw in a cartridge!" breathlessly suggested Sargent. The lever clicked, followed by a shot, which tore up the sod within a few feet of the muzzle of the rifle!

The antelope were away in a flash. Sargent rolled on the grass, laughing until the tears trickled down his cheeks, while Dell's chagrin left him standing like a simpleton.

"I don't believe this gun shoots true," he ventured at last, too mortified to realize the weakness of his excuse. "Besides, it's too easy on the trigger."

"No rifle shoots true during buck ague season," answered Sargent, not daring to raise his eyes. "When the grass comes next spring, those scars in the sod will grow over. Lucky that neither horse was killed. Honest, I'll never breathe it! Not for worlds!"

Sargent's irony was wasted. Dell, in a dazed way, recovered his horse, mounted, and aimlessly followed his bunkie. On reaching their saddles, the mental fog lifted, and as if awakening from a pleasant dream, the boy dismounted. "Did I have it?--the buck ague?" he earnestly inquired.

"You had symptoms of it," answered Sargent, resaddling his horse. "Whenever a hunter tries to shoot an empty gun, or discharges one into the ground at his feet, he ought to take something for his nerves. It's not fatal, and I have hopes of your recovery."

The two turned homeward. Several times Sargent gave vent to a peal of laughter that rang out like a rifle report, but Dell failed to appreciate the humor of the situation.

"Well," said the older one, as they dismounted at the stable, "if we have to fall back on corn beef for our Christmas dinner, I can grace it with a timely story. And if we have a saddle of venison, it will fit the occasion just as well."

The inner line was ridden at evening. The cattle were caring for themselves; but on meeting the lads from headquarters, an unusual amount of banter and repartee was exchanged.

"Killed an antelope two days before you needed it," remarked Sargent scathingly. "Well, well! You fellows certainly haven't much confidence in your skill as hunters."

"Venison improves with age," loftily observed Manly.

"That's a poor excuse. At best, antelope venison is dry meat. We located a band or two to-day, and if Dell don't care for the shot, I'll go out in the morning and bring in a fat yearling."

"Is that your prospect for a Christmas roast?" inquired Manly with refined sarcasm. "Dell, better air your Sunday shirt to-morrow and come down to headquarters for your Christmas dinner. We're going to have quite a spread."

Dell threw a glance at Sargent. "Come on," said the latter with polished contempt, reining his horse homeward. "Just as if we lived on beans at The Wagon! Just as if our porcelain-lined graniteware wasn't as good as their tin plates! Catch us accepting! Come on!"

Sargent was equal to his boast. He returned the next day before noon, a young doe lashed to his saddle cantle, and preparations were made for an extensive dinner. The practical range man is usually a competent cook, and from the stores of the winter camp a number of extra dishes were planned. In the way of a roast, on the plains, a saddle of venison was the possible extreme, and the occupants of the line-camp possessed a ruddy health which promised appetites to grace the occasion.

Christmas day dawned under ideal conditions. Soft winds swayed the dead weeds and leafless shrubs, the water trickled down the creek from pool to pool, reminding one of a lazy, spring day, with droning bees and flights of birds afield. Sargent rode the morning patrol alone, meeting Joel at the halfway point, when the two dismounted, whiling away several hours in considering future plans of the ranch.

It was high noon when the two returned to their respective quarters. Dell had volunteered to supervise the roasting of the venison, and on his crony's return, the two sat down to their Christmas dinner. What the repast lacked in linen and garnishment, it made up in stability, graced by a cheerfulness and contentment which made its partakers at peace with the world. Sargent was almost as resourceful in travel and story as Quince Forrest, and never at a loss for the fitting incident to grace any occasion.

Dell was a good listener. Any story, even at his own expense, was enjoyed. "Whether we had corn beef or venison," said he to Sargent, "you promised to tell a story at dinner to-day."

"The one that you reminded me of when you shot the rifle into the ground at your feet and scared the antelope away? No offense if I have to laugh; you looked like a simpleton."

"Tell your story; I'm young, I'll learn," urged Dell.

"You may learn to handle a gun, and make the same mistake again, but in a new way. It's live and learn. This man was old enough to be your father, but he looked just as witless as you did."

"Let's have the story," impatiently urged the boy.

"It happened on a camp hunt. Wild turkeys are very plentiful in certain sections of Texas, and one winter a number of us planned a week's shooting. In the party was a big, raw-boned ex-sheriff, known as one of the most fearless officers in the state. In size he simply towered above the rest of us.

"It was a small party, but we took along a commissary wagon, an ambulance, saddle horses, and plenty of Mexicans to do the clerking and coarse handwriting. It was quite a distance to the hunting grounds, and the first night out, we made a dry camp. A water keg and every jug on the ranch had been filled for the occasion, and were carried in the wagon.

"Before reaching the road camp, the big sheriff promised us a quail pot-pie for breakfast, and with that intent, during the afternoon, he killed two dozen partridges. The bird was very plentiful, and instead of picking them for a pot-pie, skinning such a number was much quicker. In the hurry and bustle of making the camp snug for the night, every one was busy, the sheriff in particular, in dressing his bag of quail. On finishing the task, he asked a Mexican to pour some water, and the horse wrangler reached into the wagon, at random, and emptied a small jug into the vessel containing the dressed birds.

"The big fellow adjourned to the rear and proceeded to wash and drain his quail. After some little time, he called to the cook: 'Ignacio, I smell kerosene. Look in the wagon, please, and see if the lantern isn't leaking.'

"'In a minute,' answered the cook, busy elsewhere.

"The sheriff went on washing the quail, and when about halfway through the task, he halted. 'Ignacio, I smell that kerosene again. See if the lantern isn't upset, or the oil jug leaking.'

"'Just in a minute,' came the answer as before. 'My hands are in the flour.'

"The big man went on, sniffing the air from time to time, nearly finishing his task, when he stopped again and pleadingly said: 'Ignacio, I surely smell kerosene. We're out for a week, and a lantern without oil puts us in a class with the foolish virgins. Drop your work and see what the trouble is. There's a leak somewhere.'

"The cook dusted the flour from his hands, clambered up on the wagon wheel, lifted the kerosene jug, pulled the stopper, smelt it, shook it, and lifted it above his head in search of a possible crack. The empty jug, the absence of any sign of leakage, gradually sifted through his mind, and he cast an inquiring glance at the big sheriff, just then finishing his task. Invoking heaven and all the saints to witness, he gasped, 'Mr. Charlie, you've washed the quail in the kerosene!'

"The witless, silly expression that came into that big man's face is only seen once in a lifetime," said Sargent in conclusion. "I've been fortunate, I've seen it twice; once on the face of a Texas sheriff, and again, when you shot a hole in the ground with your eye on an antelope. Whenever I feel blue and want to laugh, I conjure up the scene of a Mexican, standing on a wagon wheel, holding a jug, and a six-footer in the background, smelling the fingers of one hand and then the other."

CHAPTER XIX.
AN INDIAN SCARE

The year closed with dry, open weather. The cattle scattered wide, ranging farther afield, unmolested except by shifting winds. The latter was a matter of hourly observation, affording its lesson to the brothers, and readily explained by the older and more practical men. For instance, a north or the dreaded east wind brought the herd into the valley, where it remained until the weather moderated, and then drifted out of its own free will. When a balmy south wind blew, the cattle grazed against it, and when it came from a western quarter, they turned their backs and the gregarious instinct to flock was noticeable. Under settled weather, even before dawn, by noting the quarter of the wind, it was an easy matter to foretell the movement of the herd for the coming day.

The daily tasks rested lightly. The line was ridden as usual, but more as a social event than as a matter of necessity. The occasional reports of Manly to his employer were flattering in the extreme. Any risk involved in the existing contract hinged on the present winter, and since it was all that could be desired, every fine day added to the advantage of Wells Brothers. So far their venture had been greeted with fair winds, and with not a cloud in the visible sky. Manly was even recalled by Mr. Stoddard early in February.

Month after month passed without incident. Spring came fully a fortnight earlier than the year before. By the middle of March, the willows were bent with pollen, the birds returned, and the greening slopes rolled away and were lost behind low horizons. The line-camp was abandoned, the cattle were scattered over the entire valley, and the instincts to garden were given free rein. The building of two additional tanks, one below the old trail crossing and the other near the new camp above, occupied a month's time to good advantage. It enlarged the range beyond present needs; but the brothers were wrestling with a rare opportunity, and theirs was strictly a policy of expansion.

An occasional trip to the railroad, for supplies or pressing errand, was usually rewarded with important news. During the winter just passed, Kansas had quarantined against Texas cattle, and the trail was barred from that state. Early in May information reached the ranch that the market interests of Dodge City had moved over the line into Colorado, and had established a town on the railroad, to be known as Trail City. A feasible route lay open to the south, across No-Man's-Land, into the Texas Panhandle, while scouting parties were out with the intent of locating a new trail to Ogalalla. It would cross the Republican River nearly due westward from headquarters, and in the neighborhood of one hundred miles distant.

"There you are," said Sargent, studying a railroad folder. "You must have water for the herds, so the new market will have a river and a railroad. It simply means that the trail has shifted from the east to the west of your range. As long as the country is open, you can buy cattle at Trail City, hold them on the Colorado line until frost, and cross to your own range with a few days' travel. It may prove an advantage after all."

The blessing of sunshine and shower rested on the new ranch. The beaver ponds filled, the spill-ways of every tank ran like a mill race, and the question of water for the summer was answered. The cattle early showed the benefits of the favorable winter, and by June the brands were readable at a glance. From time to time reports from the outside world reached the brothers, and among other friendly letters received was an occasional inquiry from the commission firm, the factors named under the existing contract. The house kept in touch with the range, was fully aware of the open winter, and could easily anticipate its effects in maturing cattle for early shipment.

The solicitors of the firm, graduates of the range, were sent out a month in advance of other years. Wells Brothers were advised of a promised visit by one of the traveling agents of the commission house, and during the first week in July he arrived at headquarters. He was a practical man, with little concern for comfort, as long as there were cattle to look over. Joel took him in tow, mounted him on the pick of saddle horses, and the two leisurely rode the range.

"What does he say?" inquired Dell, after a day's ride.

"Not a word," answered Joel. "He can't talk any more than I can. Put in all day just looking and thinking. He must like cattle that range wide, for we rode around every outside bunch. He *can* talk, because he admitted we have good horses."

Again the lesson that contact teaches was accented anew. At parting the following morning, in summing up the outlook, the solicitor surprised the brothers. "The situation is clear," said he quietly. "You must ship early. Your double-wintered beeves will reach their prime this month. You may ship them any day after the 25th. Your single-wintered ones can follow in three weeks. The firm may be able to advise you when to ship. It's only a fourteen-hour run to the yards, and if you work a beef-shipping outfit that's up to date, you can pick your day to reach the market. Get your outfit together, keep in touch with the house by wire, and market your beef in advance of the glut from the Platte country."

The solicitor lifted the lines over a livery team. "One moment," said Joel. "Advise Mr. Stoddard that we rely on him to furnish us two men during the beef-shipping season."

"Anything else?" inquired the man, a memorandum-book in hand.

"Where are the nearest ranches to ours?"

"On the Republican, both above and below the old trail crossing. There may be extra men over on the river," said the solicitor, fully anticipating the query.

"That's all," said Joel, extending his hand.

The stranger drove away. The brothers exchanged a puzzled glance, but Sargent smiled. "That old boy sabes cows some little," said the latter. "The chances are that he's forgotten more about cattle than some of these government experts ever knew. Anyway, he reads the sign without much effort. His survey of this range and the outlook are worth listening to. Better look up an outfit of men."

"We'll gather the remuda to-day," announced Joel. "While I'm gone to the Republican, you boys can trim up and gentle the horses."

The extra mounts, freed the fall before, had only been located on the range, and must be gathered and brought in to headquarters at once. They had ranged in scattering bunches during the winter, and a single day would be required to gather and corral the ranch remuda. It numbered, complete, ninety-six horses, all geldings, and the wisdom of buying the majority a year in advance of their needs reflected the foresight of a veteran cowman. Many of them were wild, impossible of approach, the call of the plain and the free life of their mustang ancestors pulsing with every heart-beat, and several days would be required to bring them under docile subjection. There were scraggy hoofs to trim, witches' bridles to disentangle, while long, bushy, matted tails must be thinned to a graceful sweep.

The beginning of work acted like a tonic. The boys sallied forth, mounted on their best horses, their spirits soaring among the clouds. During the spring rains, several small lakes had formed in the sand hills, at one of which a band of some thirty saddle horses was watering. The lagoon was on the extreme upper end of the range, fully fifteen miles from headquarters;

and as all the saddle stock must be brought in, the day's work required riding a wide circle. Skirting the sand dunes, by early noon all the horses were in hand, save the band of thirty. There was no occasion for all hands to assist in bringing in the absent ones, and a consultation resulted in Joel and Dell volunteering for the task, while Sargent returned home with the horses already gathered.

The range of the band was well known, and within a few hours after parting with Sargent, the missing horses were in hand. The brothers knew every horse, and, rejoicing in their splendid condition, they started homeward, driving the loose mounts before them. The most direct course to headquarters was taken, which would carry the cavalcade past the springs and the upper winter quarters. The latter was situated in the brakes of the Beaver, several abrupt turns of the creek, until its near approach, shutting out a western view of the deserted dug-out. The cavalcade was drifting home at a gentle trot, but on approaching The Wagon, a band of ponies was sighted forward and in a bend of the creek. The boys veered their horses, taking to the western divide, and on gaining it, saw below them and at the distance of only a quarter-mile, around the springs, an Indian encampment of a dozen tepees and lean-tos.

Dell and Joel were struck dumb at the sight. To add to their surprise, all the dogs in the encampment set up a howling, the Indians came tumbling from their temporary shelters, many of them running for their ponies on picket, while an old, almost naked leader signaled to the brothers. It was a moment of bewilderment with the boys, who conversed in whispers, never halting on their course, and when the Indians reached their ponies, every brave dashed up to the encampment. A short parley followed, during which signaling was maintained by the old Indian, evidently a chief; but the boys kept edging away, and the old brave sprang on a pony and started in pursuit, followed by a number of his band.

The act was tinder to powder. The boys gave rowel to their mounts, shook out their ropes, raised the long yell, and started the loose horses in a mad dash for home. It was ten long miles to headquarters, and their mounts, already fagged by carrying heavy saddles and the day's work, were none too fresh, while the Indians rode bareback and were not encumbered by an ounce of extra clothing.

The boys led the race by fully five hundred yards. But instead of taking to the divide, the Indians bore down the valley, pursued and pursuers in plain sight of each other. For the first mile or so the loose horses were no handicap, showing clean heels and keeping clear of the whizzing ropes. But after the first wild dash, the remuda began to scatter, and the Indians gained on the cavalcade, coming fairly abreast and not over four hundred yards distant.

"They're riding to cut us off!" gasped Dell. "They'll cut us off from headquarters!"

"Our horses will outwind their ponies," shouted Joel, in reply. "Don't let these loose horses turn into the valley."

The divide was more difficult to follow than the creek. The meanderings of the latter were crossed and recrossed without halting, while the watershed zigzagged, or was broken and cut by dry washes and coulees, thus retarding the speed of the cavalcade. The race wore on with varying advantage, and when near halfway to headquarters, the Indians turned up the slope as if to verify Dell's forecast. At this juncture, a half-dozen of the loose horses cut off from the band and turned down the slope in plain sight of the pursuers.

"If it's horses they want, they can have those," shouted Joel. "Climbing that slope will fag their ponies. Come on; here's where we have the best of it."

The Indians were not to be pacified. Without a look they swept past the abandoned horses. The boys made a clear gain along a level stretch on the divide, maintaining their first lead, when the pursuers, baffled in cutting them off, turned again into the valley.

"It isn't horses they want," ventured Dell, with a backward glance.

"In the next dip, we'll throw the others down the western slope, and ride for our lives," answered Joel, convinced that a sacrifice of horses would not appease their pursuers.

The opportunity came shortly, when for a few minutes the brothers dipped from sight of the Indians. The act confused the latter, who scaled the divide, only to find the objects of their chase a full half-mile in the lead, but calling on the last reserve in their fagged horses. The pursuers gradually closed the intervening gap; but with the advantage of knowing every foot of the ground, the brothers took a tack which carried them into the valley at the old winter corral. From that point it was a straight stretch homeward, and, their horses proving their mettle, the boys dashed up to the stable, where Sargent was found at work among the other horses.

"Indians! Indians!" shouted Dell, who arrived in the lead. "Indians have been chasing us all afternoon. Run for your life, Jack!"

Joel swept past a moment later, accenting the situation, and as Sargent left the corral, he caught sight of the pursuing Indians, and showed splendid action in reaching the dug-out.

Breathless and gasping, Dell and Joel each grasped a repeating rifle, while Sargent, in the excitement of the moment, unable to unearth the story, buckled on a six-shooter. The first reconnoitre revealed the Indians halted some two hundred yards distant, and parleying among themselves. At a first glance, the latter seemed to be unarmed, and on Sargent stepping outside the shack, the leader, the old brave, simply held up his hand.

"They must be peaceful Indians," said Sargent to the boys, and signaled in the leader.

The old Indian jogged forward on his tired pony, leaving his followers behind, and on riding up, a smile was noticeable on his wrinkled visage. He dismounted, unearthing from his scanty breech-clout a greasy, grimy letter, and tendered it to Sargent.

The latter scanned the missive, and turning to the boys, who had ventured forth, broke into a fit of laughter.

"Why, this is Chief Lone Wolf," said Sargent, "from the Pine Ridge Agency, going down to see his kinsfolks in the Indian Territory. The agent at Pine Ridge says that Lone Wolf is a peaceful Indian, and has his permission to leave the reservation. He hopes that nothing but kindness will be shown the old chief in his travels, and bespeaks the confidence of any white settlers that he may meet on the way. You boys must have been scared out of your wits. Lone Wolf only wanted to show you this letter."

Sargent conversed with the old chief in Spanish, the others were signaled in, when a regular powwow ensued. Dell and Joel shook hands with all the Indians, Sargent shared his tobacco with Lone Wolf, and on returning to their encampment at evening, each visitor was burdened with pickled beef and such other staples as the cow-camp afforded.

CHAPTER XX.
HARVEST ON THE RANGE

Joel set out for the Republican the next morning and was gone four days. The beef ranches along the river had no men to spare, but constant inquiry was rewarded by locating an outfit whose holdings consisted of stock cattle. Three men were secured, their services not being urgently required on the home ranch until the fall branding, leaving only a cook and horse wrangler to be secured. Inquiry at Culbertson located a homesteader and his boy, anxious for work, and the two were engaged.

"They're to report here on the 15th," said Joel, on his return. "It gives us six men in the saddle, and we can get out the first shipment with that number. The cook and wrangler may be a little green at first, but they're willing, and that masters any task. We'll have to be patient with them--we were all beginners once. Any man who ever wrestled with a homestead ought to be able to cook."

"Yes, indeed," admitted Sargent. "There's nothing develops a man like settling up a new country. It brings out every latent quality. In the West you can almost tell a man's native heath by his ability to use baling wire, hickory withes, or rawhide."

The instinct of cattle is reliable in selecting their own range. Within a week, depending on the degree of maturity, the herd, with unerring nutrient results, turns from one species of grass to another. The double-wintered cattle naturally returned to their former range; but in order to quicken the work, any beeves of that class found below were drifted above headquarters. It was a distinct advantage to leave the herd undisturbed, and with the first shipment drifted to one end of the range, a small round-up or two would catch all marketable beeves.

The engaged men arrived on the appointed date. The cook and wrangler were initiated into their respective duties at once. The wagon was equipped for the trail, vicious horses were gentled, and an ample mount allotted to the extra men. The latter were delighted over the saddle stock, and mounted to satisfy every desire, no task daunted their numbers. Sargent was recognized as foreman; but as the work was fully understood, the concerted efforts of all relieved him of any concern, except in arranging the details. The ranch had fallen heir to a complete camp kit, with the new wagon, and with a single day's preparations, the shipping outfit stood ready to move on an hour's notice.

It was no random statement, on the part of the solicitor, that Wells Brothers could choose the day on which to market their beef. Sargent had figured out the time, either forced or leisurely, to execute a shipment, and was rather impatient to try out the outfit in actual field work.

"Suppose we break in the outfit," he suggested, "by taking a little swing around the range. It will gentle the horses, instruct the cook and wrangler, and give us all a touch of the real thing."

Joel consulted a calendar. "We have four days before beginning to gather beeves," he announced. "Let's go somewhere and camp."

"We'll move to the old trail crossing at sun-up," announced Sargent. "Roll your blankets in the morning, boys."

A lusty shout greeted the declaration. It was the opening of the beef-shipping season, the harvest time of the year, and the boys were impatient to begin the work. But the best-laid plans are often interrupted. That evening a courier reached headquarters, bearing a message from the commission firm which read, "Have your double-wintered beeves on Saturday's market."

"That's better," said Sargent, glancing over the telegram. "The wagon and remuda will start for Hackberry Grove at sun-up. Have the messenger order ten cars for Friday morning. The shipment will be on Saturday's market."

Dawn found the outfit at attention. Every movement was made with alacrity. Two men assisted a husky boy to corral the remuda, others harnessed in a span of mules, and before the sun peeped over the horizon, the cavalcade moved out up the valley, the courier returning to the station. The drag-net from below would be thrown out from the old winter corral; but as an hour's sun on the cattle rendered them lazy, half the horsemen halted until the other sighted the grove above. As early as advisable, the gradual circle was begun, turning the cattle into the valley, concentrating, and by slowly edging in, the first round-up of the day was thrown together, numbering, range run, fully six hundred head. Two men were detailed to hold the round-up compactly, Dell volunteered to watch the cut (the beeves selected), leaving the other three to cut out the marketable cattle which would make up the shipment. A short hour's work followed, resulting in eighty-odd beeves being selected. Flesh, age, and the brand governed each selection, and when cut into a class by themselves, the mettle of the pasture was reflected in every beef.

The cut was grazed up to the second round-up, which contributed nearly double the former number. On finishing the work, a count of the beeves was made, which overran in numbers the necessary shipment. They were extremely heavy cattle, twenty head to the car was the limit, and it became necessary to trim or cull back to the desired number. Sargent and Joel passed on every rejected beef, uniform weight being desirable, until the shipment stood acceptable, in numbers, form, and finish.

The beeves were watered and grazed out on their course without delay. Three days and a half were allowed to reach the railroad, and a grazing pace would land the herd in the shipping pens in good season. The day's work consisted in merely pointing and drifting the cattle forward, requiring only a few men, leaving abundant help to initiate the cook and wrangler in their field duties. Joel had been a close observer of the apparent ease with which a cook discharged his duty, frequently halting his wagon on a moment's notice, and easily preparing a meal for an outfit of trail men within an hour. The main secret lay in the foresight, in keeping his work in advance, and Joel lent every assistance in coaching his cook to meet the emergency of any demand.

Sargent took the wrangler in hand. The different bunches of horses had seen service on the trail, were gentle to handle, and attention was called to observing each individual horse and the remuda as a whole. For instance, in summer, a horse grazes against the breeze, and if the remuda was freed intelligently, at darkness, the wind holding from the same quarter during the night, a practical wrangler would know where to find his horses at dawn. The quarter of the breeze was therefore always noted, any variation after darkness, as if subject to the whim of the wind, turning the course of the grazing remuda. As among men, there were leaders among horses, and by noting these and applying hobbles, any inclination to wander was restrained. Fortunately, the husky boy had no fear of a horse, his approach being as masterly as his leave-taking was gentle and kindly--a rare gift when unhobbling alone in the open.

"I'll make a horse wrangler out of this boy," said Sargent to the father, in the presence of Dell and Joel. "Before the summer ends, he'll know every crook and turn in the remuda. There's nothing like knowing your horses. Learn to trail down the lost; know their spirit, know them in health, lame and wounded. If a horse neighs at night, know why; if one's missing in the morning, name him like you would an absent boy at school."

The trip down to the railroad was largely a matter of patience. The beeves were given every advantage, and except the loss of sleep in night-herding, the work approached loafing against time. Three guards stood watch during the short summer nights, pushing the herd off its bed at dawn, grazing early and late, and resting through the noon hours.

An agreeable surprise awaited the original trio. The evening before loading out, the beeves must be penned, and Joel rode into the station in advance, to see that cars were in waiting and get the shipping details. As if sent on the same errand, Manly met him, having been ordered on from Trail City.

"I've been burning the wires all morning," said he to Joel, "for a special train for this shipment. The agent wanted us to take a local freight from here, but I showed him there were other train shipments to follow. A telegram to the commission firm and another one to my old man done the work. Those old boys know how to pull the strings. A special train has been ordered, and you can name your own hour for leaving in the morning. I have a man with me; send us in horses and we'll help you corral your beeves."

Joel remained only long enough to confirm Manly's foresight. Two horses were sent in by Dell, and the welcome addition of two extra men joined the herd, which was easily corralled at dusk of evening. An early hour was agreed upon to load out, the empty train came in promptly, and the first shipment of the year was cut into car lots and loaded out during a morning hour.

Before the departure of the train, an air of activity was noticeable around the bleak station. The train crew was insisting for a passenger schedule, there was billing to be done and contracts to execute, telegrams of notification to be sent the commission firm, and general instructions to the beef outfit. Joel and Sargent were to accompany the shipment, and on starting, while the engineer and conductor were comparing their running orders, Sargent called out from the rear of the caboose:--

"The best of friends must part," said he, pretending to weep. "Here's two bits; buy yourself some cheese and crackers, and take some candy home to the children. Manly, if I never come back, you can have my little red wagon. Dell, my dear old bunkie--well, you can have all my other playthings."

The cattle train faded from sight and the outfit turned homeward. Horses were left at the station for Joel and Sargent, and the remainder of the outfit reached headquarters the following day. Manly had been away from the ranch nearly six months, and he and Dell rode the range, pending the return of the absent. Under ideal range conditions, the cattle of marketable age proved a revelation, having rounded into form beyond belief.

"That's why I love cattle," said Manly to Dell, while riding the range; "they never disappoint. Cattle endure time and season, with a hardiness that no other animal possesses. Given a chance, they repay every debt. Why, one shipment from these Stoddard cattle will almost wipe the slate. Uncle Dudley thought this was a fool deal, but Mr. Lovell seemed so bent on making it that my old man simply gave in. And now you're going to make a fortune out of these Lazy H's. No wonder us fool Texans love a cow."

The absent ones returned promptly. "The Beaver valley not only topped the market for range cattle," loftily said Sargent, "but topped it in price and weight. The beeves barely netted fifty-two dollars a head!"

Early shipments were urged from every quarter. "Hereafter," said Joel, "the commission firm will order the trains and send us a practical shipper. There may rise a situation that we may have to rush our shipments, and we can't spare men to go to market. It pays to be on time. Those commission men are wide awake. Look at these railroad passes, good for the year, that they secured for us boys. If any one has to go to market, we can take a passenger train, and leave the cattle to follow."

The addition of two men to the shipping outfit was a welcome asset. The first consignment from the ranch gave the men a field-trial, and now that the actual shipping season was at hand, an allotment of horses was made. The numbers of the remuda admitted of mounting every man to the limit, and with their first shipment a success, the men rested impatiently awaiting orders.

The commission firm, with its wide knowledge of range and market conditions, was constantly alert. The second order, of ten days' later date, was a duplicate of the first, with one less for fulfillment. The outfit dropped down to the old trail crossing the evening before, and by noon two round-ups had yielded twenty car-loads of straight Lazy H beeves. When trimmed to their required numbers, twenty-two to the car, they reflected credit to breeder and present owner.

In grazing down to the railroad, every hour counted. There was no apparent rush, but an hour saved at noon, an equal economy at evening and morning, brought the herd within summons of the shipping yards on time. That the beeves might be favored, they were held outside for the night, three miles from the corral, but an early sun found them safely inside the shipping pens. Two hours later, the full train was en route to market, in care of a practical shipper.

On yarding the beeves the customary telegram had been sent to the commission firm. No reply was expected, but within half an hour after the train left, a message, asking Joel to accompany the shipment, was received from Mr. Stoddard.

"You must go," said Manly, scanning the telegram. "It isn't the last cattle that he sold you that's worrying my boss. He has two herds on the market this year, one at Trail City and the other at Ogalalla, and he may have his eye on you as a possible buyer. You have a pass; you can catch the eastern mail at noon, and overtake the cattle train in time to see the beeves unloaded."

"Which herd did you come up with?" inquired Joel, fumbling through his pockets for the forgotten pass.

"With the one at Ogalalla. It's full thirty-one hundred steers, single ranch brand, and will run about equally twos and threes. Same range, same stock, as your Lazy H's, and you are perfectly safe in buying them unseen. Just the same cattle that you bought last year, with the advantage of a better season on the trail. All you need to do is to agree on the prices and terms; the cattle are as honest as gold and twice as good."

"Leave me a horse and take the outfit home," said Joel with decision. "If an order comes for more beeves, cut the next train from the Lazy H's. I'll be back in a day or two."

Joel Wells was rapidly taking his degrees in the range school. At dusk he overtook the cattle train, which reached the market yards on schedule time. The shipper's duty ceased with the unloading of the cattle, which was easily completed before midnight, when he and his employer separated. The market would not open until a late morning hour, affording ample time to rest and refresh the beeves, and to look up acquaintances in the office.

Joel had almost learned to dispense with sleep. With the first stir of the morning, he was up and about. Before the clerks even arrived, he was hanging around the office of the commission firm. The expected shipment brought the salesmen and members of the firm much earlier than usual, and Joel was saved all further impatience. Mr. Stoddard was summoned, and the last barrier was lifted in the hearty greeting between the manly boy and a veteran of their mutual occupation.

The shipment sold early in the day. An hour before noon, an interested party left the commission office and sauntered forth to watch the beeves cross the scale. It was the parting look of breeder, owner, and factor, and when the average weight was announced, Mr. Stoddard turned to the others.

"Look here, Mr. Joel," said he, "are these the cattle I sold you last summer?"

"They carry your brand," modestly admitted Joel.

"So I notice," assentingly said the old cowman. "And still I can scarcely believe my eyes. Of course I'm proud of having bred these beeves, even if the lion's share of their value to-day goes to the boys who matured them. I must be an old fogy."

"You are," smilingly said the senior member of the commission house. "Every up-to-date Texas cowman has a northern beef ranch. To be sure, as long as you can raise a steer as cheap as another man can raise a frying chicken, you'll prosper in a way. Wells Brothers aren't afraid of a little cold, and you are. In that way only, the lion's share falls to them."

"One man to his own farm, another to his merchandise," genially quoted the old cowman, "and us poor Texans don't take very friendly to your northern winters. It's the making of cattle, but excuse your Uncle Dudley. Give me my own vine and fig tree."

"Then wish the boys who brave the storm success," urged the old factor.

"I do," snorted the grizzled ranchman. "These beeves are a story that is told. I'm here to sell young Wells another herd of cattle. He's my customer as much as yours. That's the reason I urged his presence to-day."

The atmosphere cleared. On the market and under the weight, each beef was paying the cost of three the year before; but it was the letter of the bond, and each party to the contract respected his obligation.

After returning to the office, on a petty pretext, Mr. Stoddard and Joel wandered away. They returned early in the afternoon, to find all accounts made up, and ready for their personal approval. The second shipment easily enabled Joel to take up his contract, and when the canceled document was handed him, Mr. Stoddard turned to the senior member of the firm.

"I've offered to duplicate that contract," said he, "on the same price and terms, and for double the number of cattle. This quarantine raises havoc with delivery."

"A liberal interpretation of the new law is in effect," remarked the senior member. "There's too many interests involved to insist on a rigid enforcement. The ban is already raised on any Panhandle cattle, and any north of certain latitudes can get a clean bill of health. If that's all that stands in the way of a trade, our firm will use its good offices."

"In that case," said Joel, nodding to Mr. Stoddard, "we'll take your herd at Ogalalla. Move it down to the old trail crossing on the Republican, just over the state line and north of our range. This firm is perfectly acceptable again as middlemen or factors," he concluded, turning to the member present.

"Thank you," said the old factor. "We'll try and merit any confidence reposed. This other matter will be taken up with the quarantine authorities at once. Show me your exact range," he requested, turning to a map and indicating the shipping station.

Wells Brothers' range lay in the northwest corner of the state. The Republican River, in Nebraska, ran well over the line to the north, with unknown neighbors on the west in Colorado.

"It's a clear field," observed the old factor. "Your own are the only cattle endangered, and since you are the applicant for the bill of health, you absolve the authorities from all concern. Hurry in your other shipments, and the railroad can use its influence--it'll want cattle to ship next year. The ranges must be restocked."

There was sound logic in the latter statement. A telegram was sent to Ogalalla, to start the through herd, and another to the beef outfit, to hurry forward the next shipment. Joel left for home that night, and the next evening met his outfit, ten miles out from the Beaver, with a perfect duplicate of the former consignment. It was early harvest on the cattle ranges, and those who were favored with marketable beef were eager to avoid the heavy rush of fall shipments.

The beef herd camped for the night on the divide. Joel's report provoked argument, and a buzz of friendly contention, as the men lounged around the tiny camp-fire, ran through the outfit.

"It may be the custom among you Texans," protested one of the lads from the Republican, "but I wouldn't buy a herd of cattle without seeing them. Buy three thousand head of cattle unseen? Not this one of old man Vivian's boys! Oh, no!"

"Link, that kind of talk shows your raising," replied Sargent. "Your view is narrow and illiberal. You haven't traveled far. Your tickets cost somewhere between four and six bits."

Manly lifted his head from a saddle, and turning on his side, gazed at the dying fire. "Vivian," said he, "it all depends on how your folks bring you up. Down home we buy and sell by ages. A cow is a cow, a steer is a steer, according to his age, and so on down to the end of the alphabet. The cattle never misrepresent and there's no occasion for seeing them. If you are laboring under the idea that my old man would use any deception to sell a herd, you have another guess coming. He'd rather lose his right hand than to misrepresent the color of a cow. He's as jealous of his cattle as a miller is of his flour. These boys are his customers, last fall, this summer, and possibly for years to come. If he wanted them, Joel did perfectly right to buy the cattle unseen."

The second train of Lazy H beeves reached the railroad on schedule time. The shipper was in waiting, cattle cars filled the side track, and an engine and crew could be summoned on a few hours' notice. If corralled the night before, passing trains were liable to excite the beeves, and thereafter it became the usual custom to hold outside and safely distant.

The importance of restocking the range hurried the shipping operations. Instead of allowing the wagon to reach the station, at sunrise on the morning of shipping, it and the remuda were started homeward.

"We'll gather beeves on the lower end of our range to-morrow," said Joel to the cook and wrangler, "and there's no need to touch at headquarters. Follow the trail to the old crossing, and make camp at the lower tank--same camp-ground as the first shipment of Lazy H's. The rest of the outfit will follow, once these cattle are loaded out. You might have a late supper awaiting us--about ten o'clock to-night."

The gates closed on the beeves without mishap. They were cut into car lots, from horseback, and on the arrival of the crew, the loading began. A short hour's work saw the cattle aboard, when the dusty horsemen mounted and clattered into the straggling hamlet.

The homeward trip was like a picnic. The outfit halted on the first running water, and saddle pockets disgorged a bountiful lunch. The horses rolled, grazed the noon hours through, and again took up their former road gait. An evening halt was made on the Prairie Dog, where an hour's grazing was again allowed, the time being wholly devoted to looking into the future.

"If we stock the range fully this fall," said Joel, in outlining his plans, "it is my intention to build an emergency camp on this creek, in case of winter drifts. Build a dug-out in some sheltered nook, cache a little provision and a few sacks of corn, and if the cattle break the line, we can ride out of snug quarters any morning and check them. It beats waiting for a wagon and giving the drift a twenty-mile start. We could lash our blankets on a pack horse and ride it night or day."

"What a long head!" approvingly said Sargent. "Joel, you could almost eat out of a churn. An emergency camp on the Prairie Dog is surely a meaty idea. But that's for next winter, and beef shipping's on in full blast right now. Let's ride; supper's waiting on the Beaver."

CHAPTER XXI.
LIVING IN THE SADDLE

The glow of a smouldering camp-fire piloted the returning horsemen safely to their wagon. A good night's rest fitted them for the task of the day, which began at sunrise. The next shipment would come from the flotsam of the year before, many of which were heavy beeves, intended for army delivery, but had fallen footsore on the long, drouthy march. The past winter had favored the lame and halt, and after five months of summer, the bulk of them had matured into finished beef.

By shipping the different contingents separately, the brothers were enabled to know the situation at all times. No accounts were kept, but had occasion required, either Joel or Dell could have rendered a statement from memory of returns on the double and single wintered, as well as on the purchased cattle. Sale statements were furnished by the commission house, and by filing these, an account of the year's shipments, each brand separate, could be made up at the end of the season.

The early struggle of Wells Brothers, in stocking their range, was now happily over. Instead of accepting the crumbs which fell as their portion, their credit and resources enabled them to choose the class of cattle which promised growth and quick returns. The range had proven itself in maturing beef, and the ranch thereafter would carry only sufficient cows to quiet and pacify its holdings of cattle.

"If this was my ranch," said Sargent to the brothers at breakfast, "I'd stock it with two-year-old steers and double-winter every hoof. Look over those sale statements and you'll see what two winters mean. That first shipment of Lazy H's was as fat as mud, and yet they netted seven dollars a head less than those rag-tag, double-wintered ones. There's a waste that must be saved hereafter."

"That's our intention," said Joel. "We'll ship out every hoof that has the flesh this year. Nearly any beef will buy three two-year-old steers to take his place. It may take another year or two to shape up our cattle, but after that, every hoof must be double-wintered."

An hour after sunrise, the drag-net was drawing together the first round-up of the day. The importance of handling heavy beeves without any excitement was fully understood, and to gather a shipment without disturbing those remaining was a task that required patience and intelligence. Men on the outside circle merely turned the cattle on the extremes of the range; they were followed by inner horsemen, and the drag-net closed at a grazing pace, until the round-up halted on a few acres.

The first three shipments had tried out the remuda. The last course in the education of a cow-horse is cutting cattle out of a mixed round-up. On the present work, those horses which had proven apt were held in reserve, and while the first contingent of cattle was quieting down, the remuda was brought up and saddles shifted to four cutting horses. The average cow can dodge and turn quicker than the ordinary horse, and only a few of the latter ever combine action and intelligence to outwit the former. Cunning and ingenuity, combined with the required alertness, a perfect rein, coupled with years of actual work, produce that rarest of range mounts--the cutting horse.

Dell had been promised a trial in cutting out beeves. Sargent took him in hand, and mounted on two picked horses, they entered the herd. "Now, I'll pick the beeves," said the latter, "and you cut them out. All you need to do is to rein that horse down on your beef, and he'll take him out of the herd. Of course you'll help the horse some little; but if you let too many back, I'll call our wrangler and try him out. That horse knows the work just as well as you do. Now, go slow, and don't ride over your beef."

The work commenced. The beeves were lazy from flesh, inactive, and only a few offered any resistance to the will of the horsemen. Dell made a record of cutting out fifty beeves in less than an hour, and only letting one reënter the herd. The latter was a pony-built beef, and after sullenly leaving the herd, with the agility of a cat, he whirled right and left on the space of a blanket, and beat the horse back into the round-up. Sargent lent a hand on the second trial, and when the beef saw that resistance was useless, he kicked up his heels and trotted away to join those selected for shipment.

"He's laughing at you," said Sargent. "He only wanted to try you out. Just wanted to show you that no red-headed boy and flea-bit horse could turn him. And he showed you."

"This beats roping," admitted Dell, as the two returned to the herd, quite willing to change the subject. "Actually when a beef reaches the edge of the herd, this horse swells up and his eyes pop out like door-knobs. You can feel every muscle in him become as rigid as ropes, and he touches the ground as if he was walking on eggs. Look at him now; goes poking along as if he was half asleep."

"He's a cutting horse and doesn't wear himself out. Whenever you can strip the bridle off, while cutting out a beef, and handle your steer, that's the top rung a cow-horse can reach. He's a king pin--that's royalty."

A second round-up was required to complete the train-load of beeves. They were not uniform in weight or age, and would require reclassing before loading aboard the cars. Their flesh and finish were fully up to standard, but the manner in which they were acquired left them uneven, their ages varying from four to seven years.

"There's velvet in this shipment," said Sargent, when the beeves had been counted and trimmed. "These cattle can defy competition. Instead of five cents a head for watering last year's drive, this year's shipment from crumbs will net you double that amount. The first gathering of beef will square the account with every thirsty cow you watered last summer."

An extra day was allowed in which to reach the railroad. The shipment must pen the evening before, and halting the herd within half a mile of the railway corrals, the reclassing fell to Joel and Sargent. The contingent numbered four hundred and forty beeves, and in order to have them marketable, all rough, heavy cattle must be cut into a class by themselves, leaving the remainder neat and uniform. A careful hour's work resulted in seven car-loads of extra heavy beeves, which were corralled separately and in advance of the others, completing a long day in the saddle.

Important mail was awaiting Wells Brothers at the station. A permit from the state quarantine authorities had been secured, due to the influence of the commission house and others, admitting the through herd, then en route from Ogalalla. The grant required a messenger to meet the herd without delay, and Dell volunteered his services as courier. Darkness fell before supper was over and the messenger ready.

"One more shipment will clean up our beeves," said Joel to his brother, "and those through cattle can come in the day we gather our last train. We'll give them a clear field. If the herd hasn't reached the Republican, push ahead until you meet it."

A hundred-mile ride lay before Dell Wells. "You mean for the herd to follow the old trail," he inquired, "and turn off opposite our middle tank?"

"That's it; and hold the cattle under herd until we can count and receive them."

Dell led out his horse and mounted. "Dog-toe will take me safely home to-night," said he, "and we'll reach the Republican by noon to-morrow. If the herd's there, you haven't an hour to waste. We'll drop down on you in a day and a half."

The night received courier and horse. A clatter of caution and advice followed the retreating figure out of hearing, when the others threw themselves down around the camp-fire. Early morning found the outfit astir, and as on the previous occasion, the wagon and remuda were started home at daybreak. The loading and shipping instructions were merely a repetition of previous consignments, and the train had barely left the station when the cavalcade rode to overtake the commissary.

The wagon was found encamped on the Prairie Dog. An hour's rest was allowed, fresh horses were saddled, when Joel turned to the cook and wrangler: "Make camp to-night on the middle tank, below headquarters. We'll ride on ahead and drift all the cattle up the creek. Our only round-up to-morrow will be well above the old winter corral. It's our last gathering of beef, and we want to make a general round-up of the range. We'll drift cattle until dark, so that it'll be late when we reach camp."

The outfit of horsemen followed the old trail, and only sighted the Beaver late in the afternoon. The last new tank, built that spring, was less than a mile below the old crossing; and veering off there, the drag-net was thrown across the valley below it, and a general drift begun. An immense half-circle, covering the limits of the range, pointed the cattle into the valley, and by moving forward and converging as the evening advanced, a general drift was maintained. The pace was barely that of grazing, and as darkness approached, all cattle on the lower end of the range were grazed safely above the night camp and left adrift.

The wagon had arrived, and the men reached camp by twos and threes. There was little danger of the cattle returning to their favorite range during the night, but for fear of stragglers, at an early hour in the morning the drag-net was again thrown out from camp. Headquarters was passed before the horsemen began encountering any quantity of cattle, and after passing the old winter corral, the men on the points of the half-circle were sent to ride the extreme limits of the range. By the middle of the forenoon, everything was adrift, and as the cattle naturally turned into the valley for their daily drink, a few complete circles brought the total herd into a general round-up, numbering over fifteen hundred head of mixed cattle.

Meanwhile the wagon and remuda had followed up the drift, dinner was waiting, and after the mid-day meal had been bolted, orders rang out. "Right here's where all hands and the cook draw fresh horses," said Sargent, "and get into action. It's a bulky herd, and cutting out will be slow. The cook and wrangler must hold the beeves, and that will turn the rest of us free to watch the round-up and cut out."

By previous agreement, in order to shorten the work, Joel was to cut out the remnant of double-wintered beeves, Manly the Lazy H's, while Sargent and an assistant would confine their selections to the single-wintered ones in the ---- Y brand. Each man would tally his own work, even car-loads were required, and a total would constitute the shipment. The cutting out began quietly; but after a nucleus of beeves were selected, their numbers gained at the rate of three to five a minute, while the sweat began to reek from the horses.

Joel cut two car-loads of prime beeves, and then tendered his services to Sargent. The cattle had quieted, and a fifth man was relieved from guarding the round-up, and sent to the assistance of Manly. A steady stream of beef poured out for an hour, when a comparison of figures was made. Manly was limited to one hundred and twenty head, completing an even thousand shipped from the brand, and lacking four, was allowed to complete his number. Sargent was without limit, the object being to trim the general herd of every heavy, rough beef, and a tally on numbers was all that was required. The work was renewed with tireless energy, and when the limit of twenty cars was reached, a general conference resulted in cutting two loads extra.

"That leaves the home cattle clean of rough stuff," said Sargent, as he dismounted and loosened the saddle on a tired horse. "Any aged steers left are clean thrifty cattle, and will pay their way to hold another year. Turn the round-up adrift."

After blowing their horses, a detail of men drifted the general herd up the creek. Others lent their assistance to the wrangler in corralling his remuda, and after relieving the cutting horses, the beeves were grazed down the valley. The outfit had not spent a night at headquarters in some time, the wagon serving as a substitute, and orders for evening freed all hands except two men on herd with the beeves.

The hurry of the day was over. On securing fresh horses, Joel and Sargent turned to the assistance of the detail, then drifting the main herd westward. The men were excused, to change mounts, and relieved from further duty until the guards, holding the beeves, were arranged for the night. The remnant of the herd was pushed up the creek and freed near Hackberry Grove, and on returning to overtake the beeves, the two horsemen crossed a spur of the tableland, jutting into the valley, affording a perfect view of the surrounding country.

With the first sweep of the horizon, their horses were reined to a halt. Fully fifteen miles to the northeast, and in a dip of the plain, hung an ominous dust cloud. Both horsemen read the sign at a glance.

Sargent was the first to speak. "Dell met the herd on the Republican," said he with decision. "It's the Stoddard cattle from Ogalalla. The pitch of their dust shows they're trailing south."

The sign in the sky was read correctly. The smoke from a running train and the dust from a trailing herd, when viewed from a distance, pitches upward from a horizon line, and the moving direction of train or herd is easily read by an observant plainsman. Sargent's summary was confirmed on reaching headquarters, where Dell and the trail foreman were found, the latter regaling Manly and others with the chronicle of the new trail.

The same foreman as the year before was in charge of the herd. He protested against any step tending to delivery for that day, even to looking the cattle over. "Uncle Dud wouldn't come," said he, "and it's up to me to make the delivery. I've been pioneering around all summer with this herd, and now that I'm my own boss, I'll take orders from no one. We made rather a forced drive from the Republican, and I want a good night's rest for both the herd and myself. Ten o'clock in the morning will be early enough to tender the cattle for delivery. In the mean time, our pilot, the red-headed clerk, will answer all questions. As for myself, I'm going to sleep in the new tent, and if any one calls or wakes me in the morning, I'll get up and wear him out. I've lost a right smart of sleep this summer, and I won't stand no trifling."

Joel fully understood that the object in delay was to have the herd in presentable condition, and offered no objection. The beeves were grazed up opposite headquarters, and the guards were arranged for the night, which passed without incident. Thereafter, as a matter of precaution, a dead-line must be maintained between the wintered and the through cattle; and as Manly was to remain another year, he and an assistant were detailed to stay at headquarters. A reduced mount of horses was allowed them, and starting the beeves at daybreak, the wagon and remuda followed several hours later.

The trail foreman was humored in his wishes. It was nearly noon when the through herd was reached, grazed and watered to surfeiting, and a single glance satisfied Joel Wells that the cattle fully met every requirement. The question of age was disposed of as easily as that of quality.

"We gathered this year's drive on our home ranges," said the foreman, "and each age was held separate until the herds were made up. I started with fifteen hundred threes and sixteen hundred twos, with ten head extra of each age, in case of loss on the trail. Our count on leaving Ogalalla showed a loss of twelve head. I'm willing to class or count them as they run. Manly knows the make-up of the herd."

Sargent and the brothers rode back and forth through the scattered cattle. It meant a big saving of time to accept them on a straight count, and on being rejoined by the foreman, Joel waived his intent to classify the cattle.

"I bought this herd on Mr. Stoddard's word," said he, "and I'm going to class it on yours. String out your cattle, and you and Manly count against Sargent and myself."

A correct count on a large herd is no easy task. In trailing formation, the cattle march between a line of horsemen, but in the open the difficulty is augmented. A noonday sun lent its assistance in quieting the herd, which was shaped into an immense oval, and the count attempted. The four men elected to make the count cut off a number of the leaders, and counting them, sent them adrift. Thereafter, the trail outfit fed the cattle between the quartette, who sat their horses in speechless intensity, as the column filed through at random. Each man used a string, containing ten knots, checking the hundreds by slipping the knots, and when the last hoof had passed in review, the quiet of a long hour was relieved by a general shout, when the trail outfit dashed up to know the result.

"How many strays have you?" inquired Sargent of the foreman, as the quartette rode together.

"That's so; there's a steer and a heifer; we'll throw them in for good measure. What's your count?"

"Minus the strays, mine repeats yours at Ogalalla," answered Sargent, turning to Joel.

"Thirty-one hundred and ten," said the boy.

The trail foreman gave vent to a fit of laughter. "Young fellow," said he, "I never allow no man to outdo me in politeness. If you bought these cattle on my old man's word, I want you to be safe in receiving them. We'll class them sixteen hundred twos, and fifteen hundred threes, and any overplus falls to the red-headed pilot. That's about what Uncle Dud would call a Texas count and classification. Shake out your horses; dinner's waiting."

There were a few details to arrange. Manly must have an assistant, and an extra man was needed with the shipment, both of whom volunteered from the through outfit. The foreman was invited to move up to headquarters and rest to his heart's content, but in his anxiety to report to his employer, the invitation was declined.

"We'll follow up to-morrow," said he, "and lay over on the railroad until you come in with our beeves. The next hard work I do is to get in touch with my Uncle Dudley."

"Look here--how about it--when may we expect you home?" sputtered Manly, as the others hurriedly made ready to overtake the beef herd.

"When you see us again," answered Joel, mounting his horse. "If this shipment strikes a good market, we may drop down to Trail City and pick up another herd. It largely depends on our bank account. Until you see or hear from us, hold the dead-line and locate your cattle."

CHAPTER XXII.
INDEPENDENCE

The trail outfit reached the railroad a day in advance of the beeves. Shipping orders were sent to the station agent in advance, and on the arrival of the herd the two outfits made short shift in classifying it for market and corralling the different grades of cattle.

Mr. Stoddard had been located at Trail City. Once the shipment was safely within the corral, notice was wired the commission firm, affording time for reply before the shipment would leave in the morning. An early call at the station was rewarded by receipt of a wire from the west. "Read that," said the foreman, handing the telegram to Joel; "wants all three of us to come into the city."

"Of course," commented Joel, returning the message. "It's clear enough. There's an understanding between us. At the earliest convenience, after the delivery of the herd, we were to meet and draw up the final papers. We'll all go in with this shipment."

"And send the outfits across country to Trail City?"

"Throw the remudas together and let them start the moment the cattle train leaves. We can go back with Mr. Stoddard and meet the outfits at the new trail market."

"That's the ticket," said the trail boss. "I'm dead tired of riding horses and eating at a wagon. Give me the plush cushions and let me put my little feet under a table once more."

The heavy cattle train was promised a special schedule. The outfits received their orders, and at the usual hour in the morning, the shipment started to market. Weathered brown as a saddle, Dell was walking on clouds, lending a hand to the shipper in charge, riding on the engine, or hungering for the rare stories with which the trail foreman regaled the train crew. The day passed like a brief hour, the train threading its way past corn fields, country homes, and scorning to halt at the many straggling villages that dotted the route.

It was a red-letter day in the affairs of Wells Brothers. The present, their fifth shipment of the year, a total of over nineteen hundred beeves, was en route to market. Another day, and their operations in cattle, from a humble beginning to the present hour, could be condensed into a simple statement. The brothers could barely wait the intervening hours, and when the train reached the market and they had retired for the night, speculation ran rife in planning the future. And amid all their dreams and air castles, in the shadowy background stood two simple men whose names were never mentioned except in terms of loving endearment.

Among their many friends, Quince Forrest was Dell's hero. "They're all good fellows," he admitted, "but Mr. Quince is a prince. He gave us our start in cattle. Our debt to him--well, we can never pay it. And he never owned a hoof himself."

"We owe Mr. Paul just as much," protested Joel. "He showed us our chance. When pa died, the settlers on the Solomon talked of making bound boys of us. Mr. Paul was the one who saw us as we are to-day."

"I wish mother could have lived to see us now--shipping beeves by the train-load--and buying cattle by the thousand."

An eager market absorbed the beeves, and before noon they had crossed the scale. A conference, jubilant in its nature, took place during the afternoon, in the inner office of the commission firm. The execution of a new contract was a mere detail; but when the chief bookkeeper handed in a statement covering the shipments of this and the previous year, a lull in the gayety was followed by a moment of intense interest. The account showed a balance of sixty-odd thousand dollars in favor of Wells Brothers!

"Give them a letter of credit for their balance," said Mr. Stoddard, amid the general rejoicing. "And get us some passes; we're all going out to Trail City to-night. There's a few bargains on that market, and the boys want to stock their range fully."

"Yours obediently," said the old factor, beaming on his patrons. "And if the boys have any occasion to use any further funds, don't hesitate to draw on us. The manner in which they have protected their credit entitles them to our confidence. Our customers come first. Their prosperity is our best asset. A great future lies before you boys, and we want a chance to help you reach it. Keep in touch with us; we may hear of something to your advantage."

"In case we need it, can you get us another permit to bring Texas cattle into Kansas?" eagerly inquired Joel.

"Try us," answered the old man, with a knowing look. "We may not be able to, but in securing business, railroads look years ahead."

A jolly party of cowmen left for Trail City that night. Morning found their train creeping up the valley of the Arkansas. The old trail market of Dodge, deserted and forlorn-looking among the wild sunflower, was passed like a way station. The new market was only a mile over the state line, in Colorado, and on nearing their destination the party drew together.

"I've only got a remnant of a herd left," said Mr. Stoddard, "and I want you to understand that there's no obligation to even look at them. Mr. Lovell's at his beef ranch in Dakota, and his men have not been seen since the herds passed north in June. But I'll help you buy any cattle you want."

In behalf of the brothers, Joel accepted the offer. "These Texas cattle," he continued, "reach their maturity the summer following their fourth year. Hereafter, as fast as possible, we want to shape up our holdings so as to double-winter all our beef cattle. For that reason, we prefer to buy two-year-olds. We'll look at your remnant; there would be no occasion to rebrand, which is an advantage."

The train reached Trail City on time. The town was of mushroom growth--a straggling business street with fancy fronts, while the outer portions of the village were largely constructed of canvas. The Arkansas River passed to the south, numerous creeks put in to the main stream, affording abundant water to the herds on sale, while a bountiful range surrounded the market. Shipping pens, branding chutes, and every facility for handling cattle were complete.

The outfits were not expected in for another day. In the mean time, it became rumored about that the two boys who had returned with Mr. Stoddard and his trail foreman were buyers for a herd of cattle. The presence of the old cowman threw a barrier of protection around the brothers, except to his fellow drovers, who were made acquainted with his protégés and their errand freely discussed.

"These boys are customers of mine," announced Mr. Stoddard to a group of his friends. "I sold them a herd at Dodge last year, and another at Ogalalla this summer. Range on the Beaver, in northwest Kansas. Just shipped out their last train of beeves this week. Had them on yesterday's market. From what I gather, they can use about three thousand to thirty-five hundred head. At least their letter of credit is good for those numbers. Sorry I ain't got the cattle myself. They naturally look to me for advice, and I feel an interest in the boys. Their outfit ought to be in by to-morrow."

Mr. Stoddard's voucher placed the brothers on a firm footing, and every attention was shown the young cowmen. An afternoon and a morning's drive, and the offerings on the trail market had been carefully looked over, including the remnant of Mr. Stoddard. Only a few herds possessed their original numbers, none of which were acceptable to the buyers, while the smaller ones frequently contained the desired grade and age.

"Let me put you boys in possession of some facts," urged Mr. Stoddard, in confidence to the brothers. "Most of us drovers are tired out, disgusted with the slight demand for cattle, and if you'll buy out our little remnants and send us home--well, we'd almost let you name the price. Unless my herds are under contract, this is my last year on the trail."

The remnant of Mr. Stoddard's herd numbered around seven hundred head. They were largely twos, only a small portion of threes, and as an inducement their owner offered to class them at the lesser age, and priced them at the same figures as those delivered on the Beaver. On range markets, there was a difference in the selling value of the two ages, amounting to three dollars a head; and as one third of the cattle would have classed as threes, Joel waived his objection to their ages.

"We'll take your remnant on one condition," said he. "Start your outfits home, but you hang around until we make up our herd."

"That's my intention, anyhow," replied Mr. Stoddard. "My advice would be to pick up these other remnants. Two years on a steer makes them all alike. You have seen cripple and fagged cattle come out of the kinks, and you know the advantage of a few cows; keeps your cattle quiet and on the home range. You might keep an eye open for any bargains in she stuff."

"That's just what Jack Sargent says," said Dell; "that we ought to have a cow to every ten or fifteen steers."

"Sargent's our foreman," explained Joel. "He's a Texan, and knows cattle right down to the split in their hoof. With his and your judgment, we ought to make up a herd of cattle in a few days."

The two outfits came in on the evening of the fourth day. The next morning the accepted cattle were counted and received, the through outfits relieved, the remudas started overland under a detail, and the remainder of the men sent home by rail. In acquiring a nucleus, Wells Brothers fell heir to a temporary range and camp, which thereafter became their headquarters.

A single day was wasted in showing the different remnants to Sargent, and relieved of further concern, Mr. Stoddard lent his best efforts to bring buyer and seller together. Barter began in earnest, on the different fragments acceptable in age and quality. Prices on range cattle were nearly standard, at least established for the present, and any yielding on the part of drovers was in classing and conceding ages. Bargaining began on the smaller remnants, and once the buyers began to receive and brand, there was a flood of offerings, and the herd was made up the second day. The ---- Y was run on the different remnants as fast as received, and when completed, the herd numbered a few over thirty-four hundred head. The suggestion to add cows to their holdings was not overlooked, and in making up the herd, two fragments, numbering nearly five hundred, were purchased.

"The herd will be a trifle unwieldy," admitted Sargent, "but we're only going to graze home. And unless we get a permit, we had better hold over the line in Colorado until after the first frost."

"Don't worry about the permit," admonished Mr. Stoddard; "it's sure."

"We'll provision the wagon for a month," said Joel, "and that will take us home, with or without a bill of health."

The commissary was stocked, three extra men were picked up, and the herd started northward over the new Ogalalla trail. A week later it crossed the Kansas Pacific Railroad, when Joel left the herd, returning to their local station. A haying outfit was engaged, placed under the direction of Manly, and after spending a few days at headquarters, the young cowman returned to the railroad.

The expected permit was awaiting him. There was some slight danger in using it, without first removing their wintered cattle; and after a conference with Manly, it was decided to scout out the country between their range and the Colorado line. The first herd of cattle had located nicely, one man being sufficient to hold the dead-line; and taking a pack horse, Joel and Manly started to explore the country between the upper tributaries of the Beaver and the Colorado line.

A rifle was taken along to insure venison. Near the evening of the first day, a band of wild horses was sighted, the trail of which was back-tracked to a large lake in the sand hills. On resuming their scout in the morning, sand dunes were scaled, admitting of an immense survey of country, but not until evening was water in any quantity encountered. The scouts were beginning to despair of finding water for the night, when an immense herd of antelope was sighted, crossing the plain at an easy gallop and disappearing among the dunes. Following up the game trail, a perfect chain of lakes, a mile in length, was found at sunset. A venison was shot and a fat camp for the night assured.

The glare of the plain required early observation. The white haze, heat waves, and mirages were on every hand, blotting out distinct objects during the day. On leaving the friendly sand hills, the horsemen bore directly for the timber on the Republican, which was sighted the third morning, and reached the river by noon.

No sign or trace of cattle was seen. The distance between the new and old trail was estimated at one hundred miles, and judging from their hours in the saddle, the scouts hoped to reach the new crossing on the river that evening. The mid-day glare prevented observations; and as they followed the high ground along the Republican, at early evening indistinct objects were made out on the border of a distant mirage.

The scouts halted their horses. On every hand might be seen the optical illusions of the plain. Beautiful lakes, placid and blue, forests and white-capped mountains, invited the horsemen to turn aside and rest. But the allurement of the mirage was an old story, and holding the objects in view, they jogged on, halting from time to time as the illusions lifted.

Mirages arise at evening. At last, in their normal proportions, the objects of concern moved to and fro. "They're cattle!" shouted Manly. "We're near a ranch, or it's the herd!"

"Yonder's a smoke-cloud!" excitedly said Joel. "See it! in the valley! above that motte of cotton-woods!"

"It's a camp! Come on!"

The herd had every appearance of being under control. As the scouts advanced, the outline of an immense loose herd was noticeable, and on a far, low horizon, a horseman was seen on duty. On reaching the cattle, a single glance was given, when the brands told the remainder of the story.

A detail of men was met leaving camp. Sargent was among them, and after hearty greetings were over, Joel outlined the programme: "After leaving the Republican," said he, "there's water between here and home in two places. None of them are over thirty miles apart--a day and a half's drive. I have a bill of health for these cattle, and turn the herd down the river in the morning."

The new trail crossing was only a few miles above on the river. The herd had arrived three days before, and finding grass and water in abundance, the outfit had gone into camp, awaiting word from home. There was no object in waiting any great distance from headquarters, and after a day's travel down the Republican, a tack was made for the sand hills.

A full day's rest was allowed the herd on the chain of lakes. By watering early, a long drive was made during the afternoon, followed by a dry camp, and the lagoon where the wild horses had been sighted was reached at evening the next day.

It was yet early in September, and for fear of fever, it was decided to isolate the herd until after the first frost. The camp was within easy touch of headquarters; and leaving Sargent and five men, the commissary, and half the remuda, the remainder returned to the Beaver valley. The water would hold the cattle, and even if a month elapsed before frost lifted the ban, the herd would enjoy every freedom.

The end of the summer's work was in sight. The men from the Republican were paid for their services, commended for their faithfulness, and went their way. Preparations for winter were the next concern; and while holding the dead-line, plans for two new line-camps were outlined, one below the old trail crossing and the other an emergency shelter on the Prairie Dog. Forage had been provided at both points, and in outlining the winter lines, Joel submitted his idea for Manly's approval.

"Sargent thinks we can hold the cattle on twenty miles of the Beaver valley," said he, sketching the range on the ground at his feet. "We'll have to ride lines again, and in case the cattle break through during a storm, we can work from our emergency camp on the Prairie Dog. In case that line is broken, we can drop down to the railroad and make another attempt to check any drift. And as a last resort, whether we hold the line or not, we'll send an outfit as far south as the Arkansas River, and attend the spring round-ups from there north to the Republican. We have the horses and men, and no one can throw out a wider drag-net than our outfit. Let the winter come as it will; we can ride to the lead when spring comes."

The future of Wells Brothers rested on sure foundations. Except in its new environment, their occupation was as old as the human race, our heroes being merely players in a dateless drama. They belonged to a period in the development of our common country, dating from a day when cattle were the corner-stone of one fourth of our national domain. They and their kind were our pioneers, our empire builders; for when a cowman pushed into some primal valley and possessed it with his herd, his ranch became an outpost on our frontier. The epoch was truly Western; their ranges were controlled without investment, their cattle roamed the virgin pastures of an unowned land.

Over twenty-five years have passed since an accident changed the course of the heroes of this story. Since that day of poverty and uncertain outlook, the brothers have been shaken by adversity, but have arisen triumphant over every storm. From their humble beginning, chronicled here, within two decades the brothers acquired no less than seven ranches in the Northwest, while their holdings of cattle often ran in excess of one hundred thousand head. The trail passed away within two years of the close of this narrative; but from their wide acquaintance with former drovers, cattle with which to restock their ranches were brought north by rail. Their operations covered a wide field, requiring trusty men; and with the passing of the trail, their first sponsors found ready employment with their former protégés. And to-day, in the many irrigation projects of the brothers, in reclaiming the arid regions, among the directors of their companies the names of J.Q. Forrest and John P. Priest may be found.

A new generation now occupies the Beaver valley. In the genesis of the West, the cowman, the successor of the buffalo and Indian, gave way to the home-loving instinct of man. The sturdy settler crept up the valley, was repulsed again and again by the plain, only to renew his assault until success crowned his efforts. It was then that the brothers saw their day and dominion passing into the hands of another. But instead of turning to new fields, they remained with the land that nurtured and rewarded them, an equally promising field opening in financing vast irrigation enterprises and in conserving the natural water supply.

Joel and Dell Wells live in the full enjoyment of fortunes wrested from the plain. They are still young men, in the prime of life, while the opportunities of a thrifty country invite their assistance and leadership on every hand. They are deeply interested in every development of their state, preferring those avenues where heroic endeavor calls forth their best exertion, save in the political arena.

Joel Wells was recently mentioned as an acceptable candidate for governor of his adopted state, but declined, owing to the pressure of personal interests. In urging his nomination, a prominent paper, famed for its support of state interests, in a leading editorial, paid one of our heroes the following tribute:--

"... What the state needs is a business man in the executive chair. We are all stockholders in common, yet the ship of state seems adrift, without chart or compass, pilot or captain. In casting about for a governor who would fully meet all requirements, one name stands alone. Joel Wells can give M---- a business administration. Educated in the rough school of experience, he has fought his way up from a poor boy on the plains to an enviable leadership in the many industries of the state. He could bring to the executive office every requirement of the successful business man, and impart to his administration that mastery which marks every enterprise of Wells Brothers...."

The golden age is always with us. If a moral were necessary to adorn this story, it would be that no poor boy need despair of his chance in life. The future holds as many prizes as the past. Material nature is prodigal in its bounty, and whether in the grass under our feet, or in harnessing the waterfall, we make or mar our success.